D1187773

SUNSET IN THE LAND OF THE RISING SUN

INSEAD Business Press Series

SUNSET IN THE LAND OF THE RISING SUN

Why Japanese multinational corporations will struggle in the global future

J. Stewart Black
Associate Dean, Executive Development Programs, INSEAD

Allen J. Morrison
Affiliate Professor of Management, INSEAD

First published 2010 by
PALGRAVE MACMILLAN

Palgrave Macmillan in the UK is an imprint of Macmillan Publishers Limited, registered in England, company number 785998, of Houndmills, Basingstoke, Hampshire RG21 6XS.

Palgrave Macmillan in the US is a division of St Martin's Press LLC, 175 Fifth Avenue, New York, NY 10010.

Palgrave Macmillan is the global academic imprint of the above companies and has companies and representatives throughout the world.

Palgrave® and Macmillan® are registered trademarks in the United States, the United Kingdom, Europe and other countries.

ISBN: 978–0–230–25222–6

This book is printed on paper suitable for recycling and made from fully managed and sustained forest sources. Logging, pulping and manufacturing processes are expected to conform to the environmental regulations of the country of origin.

A catalogue record for this book is available from the British Library.

A catalog record for this book is available from the Library of Congress.

10 9 8 7 6 5 4 3 2 1
19 18 17 16 15 14 13 12 11 10

Printed and bound in Great Britain by
CPI Antony Rowe, Chippenham and Eastbourne

*Dedicated to our respective wives, Tanya and Angela,
for their patience and encouragement.*

CONTENTS

ILLUSTRATIONS

PREFACE

Imagine that you are a doctor and you have to tell a patient that he needs a knee **and** hip replacement. The surgery is necessary partly because of the patient's inherent predisposition for joint degradation but primarily because the patient has been a dedicated runner over the past 50 years of his life—which generally is good for one's health, except in this case. The surgery is complex and has a number of risks associated with it, from life-threatening blood clots to dangerous post-operative infections. Even if the surgery goes well and post-operative complications are avoided, you know that the patient will face months of painful physiotherapy before he can enjoy the full benefits of the surgery. However, if the complicated surgery doesn't happen, you also know that the patient is only going to get worse. In fact, you are fairly sure that within months the patient will get to the point where he will not be able to run anymore and within a year he will likely have great difficulty and experience pain just walking. Before too many years, he'll end up in a wheelchair.

As you contemplate the impending conversation with the patient, you get understandably anxious. You know the patient is going to be upset by the news. You can anticipate that he may even become angry with you as the messenger. As a consequence, it's tempting to avoid the conversation. However, not saying anything, ignoring the problem, or pretending that it doesn't exist will not magically make the knee and hip regenerate. In addition, if you don't say anything, you will deprive the patient of the opportunity to undergo the needed surgery and to make the needed changes in his lifestyle. Still, even if you go ahead with the conversation, what should you say? How should you phrase things? Should you come to the point right away or ease into the need for surgery? How much should you stress the downside of not having the surgery versus the benefits of going ahead with it? Should you focus on the surgery and say little about the post-surgery physiotherapy—its pain and duration—or should you talk about all this upfront?

While we are not medical doctors, for us this project is analogous to the physician's story. We recognize that what we say in this book may offend some Japanese executives—and even some non-Japanese executives. But just as x-rays don't lie, neither do the numbers about the standing of Japanese MNCs (Multinational Companies). Based on all the major surveys and rankings, the number of Japanese firms among the largest global players has shrunk by about half over the past 15 years. Ignoring or avoiding this fact will not magically restore Japanese firms to their glory days of the past. Sadly, our experience with many, but certainly not all, Japanese executives is that they are not that interested in hearing the facts, especially when we have employed a typical soft, implicit Japanese approach in delivering the news of their decline. This is partly why we decided to adopt a much more direct style in the book—a style that we recognize is counter-cultural for Japan and a style that for some Japanese executives might be uncomfortable. However, with 50 years of combined education and consulting experience, we have learned that sometimes when you are the bearer of bad news you have to shock patients into listening to it.

While there are benefits to taking a "shock-therapy" approach, we are well aware of the potential negative side effects, of which we want to highlight two. First, we recognize that in employing a shock-therapy approach, we run the risk that the person for whom the shock is intended will simply become more defensive and the intended message will not get through. We also recognize that such a strong approach may lead non-Japanese executives to become a bit complacent and think that they are immune to the problems that have infected a good number of Japanese firms. Obviously, we would be disappointed if either of these side effects materialized. However, the main effect of the message not getting through because of taking too soft a tone is, in our opinion, worse than either or both these potential side effects.

As a consequence, throughout this book we are going to take a fairly direct approach and put the sad facts on the table. However, we want to be clear at the outset that despite the significant decline of Japanese firms in their global standing, we do not believe that the patient is terminally ill. Much can be done to reverse the state of ailing Japanese MNCs, and we devote considerable space at the end of the book to articulate what can be done to turn things around.

Although we mentioned it already, we also want to restate that this is not just a book for Japanese executives. The patterns that we identify as so prevalent among Japanese firms can be found among firms of any and all nationalities. This is why we hope executives from various industries and counties read this book as a cautionary tale.

Finally, it is important to point out that both authors have been involved in Japan for over three decades. We are emotionally committed to the country and feel in many ways compelled to tell a story we hope will help the Japanese and other students of strategy. The lead author first went to Japan in 1978 and has lived a total of five years in the country. As a team and separately we have visited Japan regularly and worked with a variety of foreign firms operating in Japan and large Japanese firms with operations all around the world. It is this experience which brought initial interest in and admiration of the country, the culture, and the management systems of Japan. We saw and experienced first-hand the rise of Japanese firms throughout the 1980s and 1990s. This association also gave us the early glimpses into the challenges of moving from success at home and through exports to the difficulty of having operations abroad and trying to integrate those operations into a global entity.

It was after one of our visits to Japan that we decided this was a book that we had to write. We had been engaged by one of the largest, most prestigious companies in Japan to advise them on globalizing their human capital. After meeting with several dozen divisional CEOs plus corporate directors and after conducting an extensive analysis of their leadership capabilities, the time came for us to make our presentation to the group CEO. We had come well-prepared, but realized that given that it would be our first meeting we would need to go slow and leave the details for the written report. To our surprise, he wasn't the least bit interested in even listening to what we had to say. When we asked if he wanted to hear what his divisional presidents were saying, he was completely dismissive. It wasn't that he agreed or disagreed, it was just that he was more interested in telling us about his philosophy for the company than really understanding the problems his company was facing or examining solutions. During our time together, we had maybe five minutes of air-time, which was necessarily left to generalities.

We have seen this all before. We understand the importance in Japanese culture of developing relationships before people will open up, but the CEO had good international experience, limited time, and had spent a bundle of money for the report we were presenting. More worrisome is that it has now been a year since the presentation and nothing has been done to address the global leadership development needs of the company's senior executives. The CEO never read the report. No action was ever taken. If this were an exceptional case, we would be less concerned. But in our experience, this is all too common in Japan: avoid the data; push off the tough decisions; and hope the growing pains in the aging body will miraculously disappear.

While our personal experiences, often heart-felt because of our love for the Japanese people, pushed us to write this book, we trust you will find messages that inspire you to reconsider how you think about competing in the present and the future. No success, no matter how brilliant or well-earned, can last forever. It is our hope that we can learn the lessons of the past twenty years of Japanese struggles and recommit to gathering and paying attention to better data, that we can recognize anew the value of making tough, timely decisions. Just as the Japanese have recovered from far worse challenges than they face today, we should all look to a brighter future, a future of the rising, not setting, sun.

1

WHERE HAVE ALL THE FLOWERS GONE?

Even casual observers will be familiar with the Cherry Blossom or *Sakura* trees of Japan. When in full bloom, the sight is spectacular. This amazing visual is preceded by several weeks of behind-the-scenes development as the buds grow in late winter and early spring. From the time the first blossom appears (*kaika*) on a tree until the entire tree is in full bloom (*mankai*) takes only about a week. From the time of full bloom until the blossoms have all scattered (*chiru*), leaving the tree bare, also takes merely a week—sometimes less, depending on the weather.

In the longer cycle of nations and business, we see, unfortunately, a similar transitory pattern for Japanese Multinational Corporations (MNCs). After World War II, from the 1950s through 1970s, the buds of prosperity and economic impact grew for the Japanese economy and for its largest companies. In the 1980s and early 1990s, Japan and Japanese MNCs blossomed and transformed into full bloom. At this peak, the Japanese company (*kaisha*) and Japanese approach to management were the talk of the town around the world. But when the full winds of globalization blew in during the late 1990s and early 21st century, like the *sakura* blossoms after full bloom, the standing of Japanese MNCs in the world fell and their impact was scattered. More worrisome still from our perspective is that we do not see the bloom coming back for Japanese MNCs any time soon. In fact, based on our analysis, Japanese firms may fall even further unless they take serious action and make significant changes. Unfortunately, we have some doubts as to whether the needed changes will be made. We have these doubts not because of some flaw in Japan or in the Japanese executives, but because the same forces that made Japan and its companies blossom in the late 20th century are now working against them in the global future of the 21st century. In short, we see an Icarus paradox in which ironically the seeds of future failure have been sown in past success, and as we know from the Icarus story, the higher the successful flight of the past, the more likely and harder the fall in the future.

In order to get a sense of how dramatic this fall has been for Japanese firms, we merely need to look at a few numbers and charts. The first chart we want to look at shows the decline of Japanese MNCs among the *Fortune Global 500*, which ranks global companies by revenue. In 1995, the #1, #2, and #3 companies on the global list (Mitsubishi, Mitsui, and Itochu) and six of the top ten companies were all Japanese. Their domination did not stop there. A total of 37 of the top 100 *Fortune Global* firms were Japanese and 141 of the full list of 500 companies on the planet called Japan home.

By comparison, in 1995 only three of the top ten were based in the United States and only 28 (compared to Japan's 37) of the top 100 firms were from the United States. Of the full list of the *Fortune Global 500* companies, a total of 153 called the US home. For Europe the picture was similar. In 1995, only one European firm was among the ten largest (Royal Dutch Shell). A total of 38 European firms were ranked among the top 100 and a total of 155 of the full *Fortune Global 500* were based in Europe.

Whether 1995 was *mankai* (or peak blossom) for Japan is a little hard to tell because 1995 was the first year that *Fortune* combined service and manufacturing companies to create its "Global 500" list. However, evidence suggests that 1995 may well have been the peak because Japanese MNCs experienced steady decline thereafter. In fact, in the thirteen years that ensued, like the *sakura* blossoms after full bloom, the share of Japanese companies in the *Fortune Global 500* has dropped dramatically.

Whereas in 1995 the Japanese occupied six of the top ten spots, by 2008 the number had declined by 83% and only one Japanese firm (Toyota) was counted among the ten. While in 1995 a total of 37 Japanese firms were ranked among the "Top 100," by 2008 the number had declined by 78%, leaving only eight companies in the list!

In contrast, during this time both US and European firms fared much better. In the Top 10, the number of US firms increased from 3 to 5 and the number of European firms increased from 1 to 4. In addition, in the Top 100, the number of US firms increased from 28 to 31, while the number of European firms decreased only by one, from 38 to 37. These changes in the top 100 *Fortune* firms are illustrated in Exhibit 1.1 and Exhibit 1.2.

While Exhibit 1.1 looks at the decline of Japanese firms in the top 100, Exhibit 1.2 looks at the decline of Japanese firms within the full

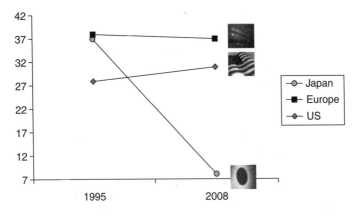

EXHIBIT 1.1 **Decline of Japanese MNCs among** *Fortune Global 100* **(1995–2008)**
Source: *Fortune Global 500* List 1995, 2008.

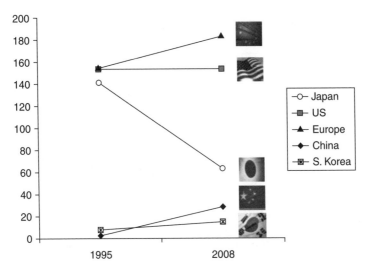

EXHIBIT 1.2 **Decline of Japanese MNCs among** *Fortune Global 500* **(1995–2008)**
Source: *Fortune Global 500* List 1995, 2008.

Fortune Global 500. In 1995, there were 141 Japanese firms in the Top 500, by 2008 that number had declined by more than 50% to 64 companies or it could be said, from a 28.2% share to a 12.8% share of the total. In contrast, the total US firms in the Top 500 stayed the same at 153. The number of European firms in the Top 500 increased from 154 to 183. This period between 1995 and 2008 also saw a noticeable increase of firms from developing countries such as Korea and China in the Global 500.

Based on these data, it seems that the standing of Japanese MNCs has, like expired cherry blooms, fallen dramatically. However, during a presentation of this data to a team of senior managers at a major Japanese multinational company, a Japanese executive challenged the implications. His point was that even if the overall percentage of Japanese firms has dropped, if Japanese firms are the global leaders within their industries, then their effective standing would not be as low as it would otherwise seem. This seemed like a fair point, so we looked more deeply into the data.

Specifically, we examined the 2008 *Fortune Global 500* list because it provided segmentation by industry. The segmentation enabled us to see if Japanese firms had lost their standing across most industries or whether the decline was explained by tough times in just a few industries. *Fortune* divides the Global 500 firms into 51 different industries and ranks the firms within each industry. We looked within each industry and tabulated the "nationality" of the #1 ranked firm in that industry. Exhibit 1.3 details these findings and illustrates that Japanese firms lag significantly behind the US, German and French MNCs.

The Japanese executive then rightly asked if these numbers reflected the overall size of the countries. After all, one would generally expect countries with larger economies to have a higher proportion of large, global companies. Indeed, GDP rankings of these countries provide some insight as to what you might expect in terms of how MNCs from each of the countries ought to stack up. Exhibit 1.4 provides the International Monetary Fund's ranking of the top 6 countries plus Switzerland, which is ranked 21st.

Based on Exhibit 1.4, if countries held a relative share of the #1 industry ranking in the *Fortune Global 500* similar to their overall GDP

EXHIBIT 1.3 **Nationality of #1 Ranked Firms within Each Industry for the** *Fortune Global 500*

Nationality	Total #	% of Total
US	27	52.9
Germany	5	9.8
France	5	9.8
Japan	3	5.9
Switzerland	2	3.9
Other	9	17.7

Source: *Fortune Global 500* List 2008.

EXHIBIT 1.4 **Size and Share of Country GDP**

Rank	Country	GDP (millions of USD)	Share of World GDP (%)
—	*World*	*54,584,918*	100
—	EU	16,905,620	31
1	US	13,840,000	25
2	*Japan*	*4,381,576*	*8*
3	Germany	3,320,913	6
4	China (PRC)	3,280,224	6
5	UK	2,804,437	5
6	France	2,593,779	5
21	Switzerland	427,074	1

Source: International Monetary Fund Data and Statistics 2007.

ranking and relative share, you could expect Japan to have about 1/3 (or more precisely 32%) as many firms in the #1 ranking as the United States (or conversely you might expect the United States to have about 3 times as many #1 firms as Japan). You could also expect Japan to have more #1 ranked firms than either Germany or France. However, Japan has three #1 firms compared to the United States' 27, which is about 11% of the United States' total—not the 32% you would expect based on GDP size. In other words, the United States has 9 times as many #1 ranked firms as Japan rather than the 3 times you would expect. Also, both Germany and France have over 1.5 times as many #1 ranked firms as Japan—not fewer as you would expect. Interestingly, Switzerland had the 5th most #1 ranked firms in the *Fortune Global 500* even though it is ranked only 21st in terms of GDP. And thus, where you might have expected Japan to have 10 times as many #1 ranked firms as Switzerland based on relative GDP size, Japan has only 1.5 times as many. All of these data suggests that Japan is now punching well below its GDP weight in terms of global powerhouse firms and Switzerland is punching well above its weight.

As we mentioned, the *Fortune Global 500* ranking is based on revenues. While revenues are a good proxy for size and heft, they are not the only means of measuring the ranking of firms across the global landscape. The United Nations takes a somewhat different approach and looks more at the foreign asset base of companies and then ranks the top 100 (see Exhibit 1.5). Even though the United Nations (United Nations Conference on Trade and Development, UNCTAD) looks at asset value rather than revenue and ranks only the top 100 not the top 500 firms, we still see a similar picture in Exhibit 1.5 as we saw in Exhibit 1.2. We see a 50% decline in the number of top-ranked

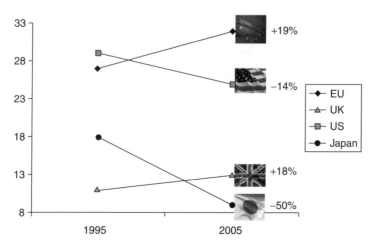

EXHIBIT 1.5 Change in Top 100 Transnational Firms by Country (1995–2005)
Source: UNCTAD Transnational Corporation Rankings 1995 and 2005.

Japanese firms between 1995 and 2005 (the most recent data available at the time of printing). As with the *Fortune* rankings, the number of European firms in the UNCTAD Top 100 increased between 1995 and 2005. This trend was particularly true for British firms. In contrast, the number of US firms in the UNCTAD Top 100 declined slightly between 1995 and 2005. However, the decline among the Japanese firms was significant.

When we dig deeper into the UNCTAD 2005 rankings, we find more evidence to prove the point that Japanese firms have not kept pace with firms from other countries in terms of global growth and expansion. Specifically, Exhibit 1.6 illustrates that even though Japan's economy is roughly 25% larger than that of Germany or France and more than 50% bigger than the United Kingdom's, Japan has about 40% fewer companies in the UNCTAD Top 100 ranking than Germany, France, or the United Kingdom.

If one takes a very different view and focuses neither on revenues as *Fortune* does nor on tangible assets as the United Nations, but on intangible asset value, what does the picture look like? Arguably one of the most important intangible assets in the modern age is brand and brand value. Unfortunately, it is more difficult to precisely compare changes in Japanese companies' global standing on brand value over the same time frame as we tracked their standing by revenues and by assets. It is virtually impossible to find a systematic and comprehensive tracking of global brands and global brand value that goes back

EXHIBIT 1.6 **UNCTAD Top Ranked Transnational Firms by Country 2005**

Rank	Nationality of Firm	Total # in Top 100
1	US	25
2	UK	13
2	France	13
4	Germany	12
5	Japan	9
6	Switzerland	4
7	Netherlands	3
7	Italy	3

Source: UNCTAD Transnational Corporation Rankings 2005.

EXHIBIT 1.7 **Ranking of Countries by Top 100 Global Brands**

Country	2001	2008
US	1	1
Germany	2	2
France	4 (tie)	3
Japan	3	4
Switzerland	4 (tie)	5
UK	6	6

Source: Interbrand Best Global Brands 2001, 2008.

beyond 2001. Consequently, while we can look at comparisons on revenues and assets over the past 14 years, for assessments of brand value, we can look back only over the past 7 years.

In making this analysis of brand value over time, we used Interbrand, which is arguably the authority on the value and ranking of global brands. Based on their data, when we look at the relative standing of Japanese companies' brand value over time, an unhealthy picture emerges. As Exhibit 1.7 illustrates, over the past several years, American and German companies have held on to their #1 and #2 rankings respectively in terms of the number of brands in the Top 100, but Japan has lost its #3 ranking to France.

If you look at not just the number of brands in the Top 100, but at the value of those brands, we see additional bad news for Japanese companies. Exhibit 1.8 provides a ranking of the countries by the total

EXHIBIT 1.8 **Ranking of Countries by Total Value ($ in millions) among Top 100 Global Brands**

	2001	2008	Percentage change
US	739,703	778,109	0.05
Germany	55,692	98,609	0.77
Japan	67,751	94,229	0.39
France	13,788	84,905	5.16
UK	14,036	74,168	4.28
Switzerland	17,955	43,257	1.41

Source: Interbrand Best Global Brands 2001, 2008.

value of their brands in the Global Top 100 as computed by Interbrand. Based on Interbrand's 2001 and 2008 data, we see that both the trends and recent standings are not good for Japanese firms. First, although the United States' 2008 GDP was only 3 times that of Japan, the brand value of US MNCs was 8 times higher. In addition, even though Japan's GDP was 25% bigger than France's or Germany's, Japanese firms' brand value was about 5% smaller than German firms' value (not bigger) and was only 10% greater than French firms' brand value (not 25%). Furthermore, even though Japan's economy was 10 times bigger than Switzerland's, the brand value of Japanese companies was just over 2 times as great. Finally, all of the countries' growth in brand value over this period significantly outpaced that of Japan, with the exception of the United States, which was growing from a much higher base value.

SUMMARY

We stated at the outset of this chapter that Japanese companies were showing serious signs of losing their standing in the landscape of global players. The data illustrate the magnitude of this decline. Obviously there are variety of questions these findings provoke, from "How did this happen?" to "What should Japanese executives do about it?" The key questions we address in each subsequent chapter are highlighted below:

- **Chapter 2**: "What were the forces that enabled Japan and Japanese companies to blossom at home?"
- **Chapter 3**: "What were the forces that enabled Japan and Japanese companies to blossom abroad through exports?"

- **Chapter 4**: "What is so different about the global stage of development that seems to be causing Japanese MNCs trouble in the 21st century?"
- **Chapter 5**: "How have Japanese MNCs struggles in early overseas operations hurt their ability to move forward toward greater globalization?"
- **Chapter 6**: "Why have Japanese companies struggled finding and developing non-Japanese leaders for their international operations?"
- **Chapter 7**: "Why have Japanese companies struggled with innovation outside of Japan?"
- **Chapter 8**: "What does this relative rise and fall look like at ground level for an individual manager?"
- **Chapter 9**: "Why can't Japanese companies just ignore all this and focus on Japan and still be successful going forward?"
- **Chapter 10**: "What can Japanese executives do to escape the current freefall?"
- **Chapter 11**: "What can others learn from this tale and what can they do to ensure they prosper in a global future?"

In closing out this chapter, we want to reiterate that while we see systemic and structural forces that will make it very difficult for most Japanese firms to prosper in a global 21st century, the future is not predestined; every Japanese firm is not doomed to a future of perpetual decline. Change is possible and we will highlight some Japanese firms that have broken the code for leveraging the past while not being limited by it and seem to be set for bright prospects in the future.

2

FOLLOW THE YELLOW BRICK ROAD, PART 1

In Chapter 1, we highlighted how far Japanese MNCs have fallen. But to fall you first have to rise. As a consequence, you naturally wonder, "How did Japanese MNCs rise so high?" You might also wonder, "Even if Japanese MNCs have fallen, can they get up?" In order to answer these key questions, we need to step back and view things from a broader perspective. That is, we need to look at Japanese MNCs within a common pattern of global corporate evolution and strategy.

Therefore, in this chapter, we first provide some background on patterns of MNC evolution and look at how company strategy changes as firms push forward along the path to globalization. While the path to globalization is not quite as singular as the yellow brick road to the Land of Oz, it turns out that there is a commonly trodden path to globalization. Once we understand the common path, we can then take a look at what contributed to the rise of Japanese companies on the early portion of that path, which will be the focus of this chapter and the next.

THE PATH TO GLOBALIZATION

Our academic friends might argue that the nice and neat picture we are about to paint for you is perhaps too simple. They might also want to point out the exceptions to the pattern that we will present. From our perspective, that's OK. Most business people we have worked with in our combined 50+ years of consulting live by the 80/20 rule. That is, they want to know the 20% of factors that account for 80% of the outcome. In their minds, the few exceptions actually prove the rule and justify why the rule, rather than the exception, is worth paying attention to. We agree.

In keeping with the 80/20 principle, Figure 2.1 captures a pattern that the majority of firms follow as they move from a domestic business to a borderless and global enterprise. It suggests that at the most

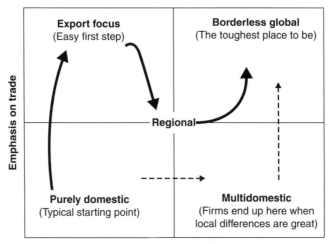

Figure 2.1 **Stages on the Path of Globalization**

fundamental level, firms have only two tools at their disposal when it comes to international business. They can either export/trade or invest in the overseas market.[1] Trade includes the flow of not just products but also of knowledge and expertise. Foreign Direct Investment (FDI) includes money to build factories, distribution centers, warehouses, etc. Trade and FDI are the primary building blocks of international business strategy and competition.

In an effort to shorten and simplify what otherwise could be a long and complicated discussion, we first briefly walk through the common four stages companies go through as they shift from a domestic focus to a borderless, global orientation. We then touch on the important exceptions to this common pattern. Finally, we dive into greater detail on the factors that facilitated the rise of large Japanese firms during the stage of development when they were domestically focused. In Chapter 3, we dive into the factors that facilitated their rise as exporters.

FOUR STAGES ON THE PATH TO GLOBALIZATION

Stage 1: Domestic focus

Virtually all companies start with a strong domestic focus. In the past, companies were not only born in their home country but largely competed against firms that were also born in and focused on the home market—that is, domestic competitors. This certainly was true of Japan during all of the 20th century. Even today it is still largely the case.

Stage 2: Exports

When you are successful at home, you quite naturally start thinking, "Why can't I export some of this success to other markets?" In fact, the more demanding the competitive conditions of the domestic market, especially in terms of customers and competitors, the more likely it is that you in fact have products that customers in other markets will want and that competitors in those market will have a hard time matching in terms of quality, price, or some combination thereof.

Having achieved success at home, most firms focus first on exports rather than jumping straight into setting up shop all around the world for solid economic reasons. One of the most powerful factors is the unit cost and margin enhancing benefits of capturing economies of scale by utilizing existing assets at home. Unless the product has a terrible weight-to-value ratio, such as bricks or cement, or spoils easily, like fresh bread, the shipping costs associated with exporting are often offset by the savings captured through economies of scale. And if a product, such as a watch or a microprocessor, has a great value-to-weight ratio, then shipping costs are typically minimal compared to the benefits of producing more from your existing assets and exporting the product around the world.

Stage 3: Regional focus

To the dismay of die-hard exporters, most firms discover that as you expand geographic coverage and offer your products to more and more customers in an increasing number of places, you run into three inconvenient but related facts. First, many customers are not the same the world over. Second, many of these foreign customers are not the same as your domestic customers. Third, below the layer of "easy export acceptors" is typically a much larger group of customers for whom the first two facts relate. These customers have higher demands for service, require better treatment, insist on more customized products, etc. Customers like this tend to ask questions such as: Can the exporter guarantee delivery by building a warehouse close to the port? Can they speed repairs by carrying them out locally? Can they provide manuals and instructions and offer help desk services in the local language? Can they add a local product development team to work with us to ensure that the OEM products produced back in the supplier's home country are better suited for our local consumers? Can they do more to support their products through local advertising? Can they purchase some components locally? The list goes on. And who could argue with the logic of these requests? They all seem reasonable—even inevitable.

If an exporting company wants to continue to grow revenues by broadening and deepening its foreign customer base, it has little choice but to respond to these localization requirements. Some studies suggest that scale economies often max out at regional—not global—production levels.[2] So regional strategies have the potential to be relatively efficient. Indeed, evidence suggests that most FDI is quite regionalized.[3] However, by definition moving out of the export stage and into the regional stage requires some "localization." For the evolving MNC, this means moving away from the core domestic practices with which it grew up.

Stage 4: Borderless global business

The transition into and the realities of borderless global competition are marked by the reemergence of two dynamics that separately played leading roles in the export and regional stages of company evolution. In the export stage, the economies of scale and benefits of standardization pushed companies to focus on making something one way at home and then selling the same product around the world. In the regionalization stage, the differences across regions and countries pushed companies to begin to modify and adapt products and services to the local differences. In the borderless global stage both forces—the forces for global integration *and* for local adaptation—simultaneously hold sway. As a consequence, companies struggle with and eventually must master a complex process of determining which things to globally integrate, which things to locally differentiate, and which activities and products to have unique blends of both.

Therefore, a borderless global strategy does NOT mean that the company does everything the same around the world. It also does NOT mean that it "thinks global and acts local," which has become a common buzz phrase. It *does* mean that some things are globally integrated and standardized in thought *and* action, while some are locally differentiated in thought *and* action. It also means that there are still other things that are a hybrid or blend of both.

What makes the firm borderless and global is that all activities are viewed in their global totality. Borderless global competitors lose their tight loyalty to their home countries, and they care more about global positioning, market share, competitiveness, etc. than about single market positions. By thinking about the world in its entirety, they are better able to learn about best practices, and by caring less about nationality, they are better able to internalize knowledge gained wherever in the world they find it and disseminate it wherever in the world they need it. It is from this comprehensive perspective that executives determine what is the right level or mix of global integration and local responsiveness.

EXCEPTIONS TO THE RULE

As we pointed out at the beginning of this chapter, there are exceptions to the overall pattern of globalization, and now we want to briefly touch on the three most common.

First, clearly not all companies globalize, nor should they. Many small and even some medium-sized businesses remain pure domestic players their entire lives. Nothing is necessarily wrong with this, although as we discuss later, staying a successful locally focused competitor has its own challenges.

Second, in a few exceptional cases, like Indian software service firms, some companies leap-frog from exporting to borderless global strategies without really passing through the regional stage.[4] But this is extremely rare.

Third, some companies move from a pure domestic to multidomestic orientation and skip the export stage. A multidomestic orientation is characterized by having multiple foreign operations, but each foreign unit is almost exclusively focused on the domestic market in which that unit is located. While a few firms remain with a multidomestic orientation, the liberalization of trade eventually pushes most to move toward a borderless, global orientation.

JAPAN BEFORE WORLD WAR II

With this general context in mind, we can now take a look at the evolution of Japanese MNCs. As we examine the rise of Japanese companies in their home market, we need to step back just a bit in time. While the post–World War II rise of Japan is critical to the rise of Japanese MNCs, we need to appreciate that the modern Japanese MNC traces its roots a bit further back to the *Meiji* Restoration, beginning in 1868 or just over 70 years before the start of World War II. Meiji, the "enlightened rule," describes the Japanese government's efforts to blend the best of Japanese culture and tradition with Western economic and technological advancements.[5] During this period, power was consolidated under the Emperor and shogunate and samurai were essentially eliminated.[6] With relative political stability and an opening to the West, Japan experienced remarkable growth. In 1873, for example, the size of Japan's merchant fleet was 26 ships; by 1913, it reached 1,514 vessels. Between 1875 and 1913, coal production increased from 600 thousand metric tons to 21.3 million metric tons. Roads were built, factories created, and train lines were extended throughout much of the country. It was also during this period that the Japanese Imperial Army gained stature and tightened its relationship with the Emperor.

It is also worth pointing out that Japan participated in World War I as an ally of Britain, and after the Americans entered the War in 1917, with the United States. It declared war on Germany in 1914 and occupied a number of German territories in Asia during the War. It sent war ships to South Africa and the Mediterranean. It was also during this period that Japan occupied parts of Manchuria, followed by a full invasion of northeastern China in 1931.

The rapid growth of the Japanese economy in the latter part of the 19th century and early 20th century helps remind us that Japan was a growing power even before it had to rise from the ashes of World War II. Much of what was put in place in the years before World War II contributed significantly to the country's ability to recover. No doubt, the self-image of many Japanese as successful, prosperous people developed over many decades of economic growth contributed to their speedy recovery after World War II.

The rise of the "Land of the Rising Sun," both during the Meiji Restoration and after World War II, has been chronicled by many authors and is recorded in dozens of books,[7] so there is no need for us to go into great detail here; however, we do need to cover some of the basics.

STAGE 1: DOMESTIC BIRTH AND FOCUS

As illustrated in Figure 2.1, the first stage on the path to globalization is a domestic focus. Until recently, it was virtually impossible for a firm to be born global. Most of today's biggest firms, were started 30, 40, and many over 100 years ago. Nearly every one of them was born or established in one particular country. For example, General Electric was born in the United States, Michelin in France, and Toyota was started in Japan. Not only are most companies born in a single country but they also spend their infant, toddler, and adolescent years primarily in their "birth country." Similar to a young child, companies too are influenced by the language, culture, customs, and practices that surround them. In business, the equivalent of influential parents, friends, and neighbors are customers, competitors, employees, suppliers, regulators, and shareholders (see Figure 2.2).

There is nothing remarkable about this simple model of business constituencies presented in Figure 2.2. However, because the domestic dynamics vary from country to country, it is important to briefly walk through the model to remind ourselves of how different customers, competitors, employees, suppliers, regulators, and shareholders can be from one country to another.

For example, simply consider how in Japan unions are basically limited to enterprises, while in the United States they are typically organized

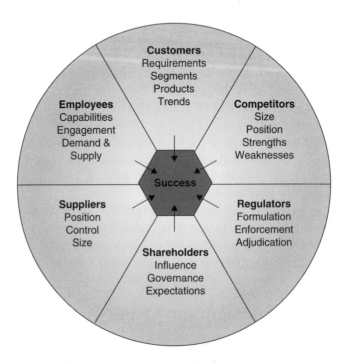

Figure 2.2 **Key Constituencies for Success**

across companies. This means, in Japan the unions cannot leverage the power of national membership numbers and as a consequence their interests are naturally more closely tied to those of the company in which union members work. In the United States, unions can easily leverage their national membership numbers and financial resources in negotiating with just one company. For example, in the United States, the United Auto Workers' Union (UAW) has a total of just over 500,000 members across 2,000 different companies.[8] This means that the UAW has a national base of member fees that allows it to support a strike against a given company for much longer than the union employees of that one company could ever do on their own. This simple difference alone can in turn affect management-labor relations, negotiation philosophy and style, and even the likelihood of moving jobs offshore. Does this one difference explain all the differences between Toyota and Ford? Of course not. But it reminds us that Ford would not look as it does now if it grew up in Japan, and Toyota would have a different approach to business in general and labor-management relations in particular if it had been born and raised in Detroit.

With this reminder, we can jump to a three-part axiom relative to this first step along the path to globalization—an axiom that has critical implications along the entire globalization journey:

1. the more different the home environment is from other markets,
2. the more successful the company is at home, and
3. the longer the domestic company stays focused on its domestic market and the longer it enjoys domestic success,

    the more difficulty the company will experience transitioning from the early to the later stages on the path to globalization.

As we will see throughout this book, this axiom is particularly relevant to Japanese firms. The starting point of Japanese firms' current difficulty lies primarily in their past success at home, mastering the six core constituencies and in how different the core constituencies in Japan were from those same constituencies in other countries.

Customers

The first constituency that Japanese companies mastered was their customers. What is important to appreciate here is that for the most part

Japanese customers are not easy to please and by most accounts are some of the most demanding customers on the planet. Michael Dell noted this recently when he opened Dell's Miyazaki Customer Center in Japan (March 22, 2007) by saying, "you [the Japanese] are the most demanding customers we have in the world...and I mean that as a compliment." These demanding Japanese customers helped Japanese companies become better. However, it is important to appreciate that not only were Japanese customers demanding but they were also willing to pay for the nuanced and extra features they desired. To understand this easily and quickly, you only need to go to a typical grocery store in Japan and head over to the fruit and vegetable section. Take a look at the strawberries or the apples. They will be perfect—fresh, no blemishes, precisely arranged, and nearly uniform in size, shape, and color. For this perfection, they will on average cost about 20–40% more than the same fruit in the United States, Germany, or France. In general, you won't find this same level of perfection in most American or European stores. Why? Are American and European fruit growers inferior to Japanese farmers? Not at all. The difference lies in consumer preferences. When it comes to a fruit, American, European, and Japanese consumers all value freshness. However, American and European consumers are just not as demanding as the Japanese on some of the other dimensions. Or precisely, they do not see the same value for money in these *small* points of perfection such as uniform size or precise arrangement on the shelf. As a Spanish consumer, do I really care if the stems of the apples are all pointing in exactly the same direction? And even if I did care, do I care enough to pay extra for it? In contrast, Japanese customers do care. In fact, because they are willing to pay for the apple stems pointing in the exact same direction and for the apples to all be essentially the same size, color, etc., these differences to Japanese consumers are not small.

Competitors

Depending on where a firm is born today, it might have to compete with both domestic and foreign adversaries. This was not so much the case 50 years ago in most countries and certainly not in Japan. As we will document in detail in the next chapter, Japan did not attract significant foreign investment from the 1960s through the 1990s. In fact, in 1976, there were 1,101 foreign firms operating in Japan. Twenty years later, there were only 1,421 foreign firms operating in Japan—a net increase of only 320 foreign firms in 20 years.[9]

Beyond looking at sheer volume data, how different can competition and competitors be from one country to another? To illustrate this, let's look just briefly at the Honda-Yamaha motorcycle war in the 1980s.[10] In January 1982, Honda's President Kawashima declared, "Yamaha has not only stepped on the tail of a tiger, it has ground it into the earth. As long as I am president of this company, we will surrender our number one position to no one. *Yamaha wo tsubusu!* [Crush, break, smash, destroy Yamaha!]"

What had Yamaha done to ignite the wrath of Honda? To answer this question, we have to go back to the early 1950s when there were 50 domestic competitors fighting for position in the Japanese motorcycle market. The number one firm was Tohatsu with a 22% market share and Honda was number two with a 20% share. From 1955 to 1960, Honda grew aggressively but Tohatsu did not. Honda's aggressive moves during this period helped its market share to more than double and shoot from 20% to 44%, while Tohatsu's shrank from 22% to 4%. Four years later, in 1964, Tohatsu filed for bankruptcy. By 1965, only 4 out of 50 original competitors were left—Honda, Yamaha, Suzuki, and Kawasaki.

At that point, Honda was king of the two-wheeled domestic kingdom. Not content, over the next 15 years, Honda expanded from two-wheeled vehicles to four-wheeled vehicles. In 1979, President Koike of Yamaha saw a competitive opening for his firm against Honda. He stated, "At Honda, sales attention is focused on four-wheel vehicles. Most of their best people in motorcycles have been transferred [into cars]. Compared to them, our specialty at Yamaha is mainly motorcycle production." In August 1981, Yamaha announced plans to construct a new motorcycle factory with an annual capacity of one million units. This new factory plus its existing capacity would give Yamaha a total capacity of more than 200,000 units greater than that of Honda. Assuming Yamaha could sell all its units, it would surpass Honda and capture 60% of the total market. At the Yamaha annual shareholder's meeting, Yamaha president Koike declared, "In one year we will be the domestic leader, and in two years, we will be number one in the world."

This was effectively a war declaration and, in fact, a war between Honda and Yamaha ensued. Honda, however, was determined not to lose and so executives rapidly redeployed forces, increased production capacity, and launched 81 new models over the next 12 months compared to 17 new models in the previous 12 months. Yamaha tried to respond but was able to launch only 34 new models. By 1983, Yamaha's unsold stock of motorcycles in Japan was estimated to be half of the total industry's unsold stock. In February, president Koike of Yamaha committed figurative *seppuku* (ritual suicide) by publically apologizing:

> *We cannot match Honda's product development or sales strength...and would like to end the Honda-Yamaha war...moving cautiously toward a cooperative stance with other companies ensuring Yamaha's relative position.*

With that apology, the war ended. Honda retained its number one position and Yamaha never again tried to step out of place in Japan. Perhaps this is not completely unique to Japan, but it is hard to point to many other countries where a public apology for being competitive stopped a war and created a peace accord that lasted another 30 years. This was possible in Japan because both firms were Japanese, steeped in its traditions and culture, including the modern form of corporate *seppuku*—the public apology of the top corporate official—which then allows all previous offenses to be forgiven.

Employees

During these formative years when Japanese firms focused on the domestic market, it should come as no surprise that Japanese firms dealt almost exclusively with Japanese employees. While individual Japanese may resent the notion that they are a more rather than less homogeneous people, the facts are the facts. For example, if you conduct a survey and ask about core cultural values such as orientation toward groups or individuals, toward avoiding or embracing risk, or toward endorsing or simply tolerating hierarchy, you can subsequently compute average responses within a country. Studies have found that not only are Japanese more group-oriented, more risk adverse, and more endorsing of hierarchical difference than say Americans or Dutch but also the Japanese have smaller variations around their averages.[11] So while we do not want to create the impression that all Japanese workers are clones, a common history, language, ethnicity, culture, and very low level of foreign immigration have contributed to a more cohesive and uniform set of employees for Japanese companies when compared to domestic employees in other countries. The point here is that during their domestic years Japanese firms became very good at managing Japanese employees. Because these employees were more similar than different, the Japanese had little experience managing diversity.

Suppliers

The supplier relationships that Japanese firms mastered domestically were also somewhat unique. For example, the *keiretsu* system had a distinctive and powerful impact on supplier relationships in Japan.[12] Companies in the post–World War II *keiretsu* system followed similar patterns established by the pre-World War II military conglomerates known as the *zaibatsu*, which were dismantled by General Douglas MacArthur after the war. The *keiretsu* included interlocking ownerships in a wide range of companies. At the center was typically a combination of three core companies: a city bank, a trading company—the *sogo shosha*—and a manufacturer, for example a steel company or automobile assembler. From the center, tentacles of tiered relationships with affiliated companies reached out, providing support to the broader network. In some cases, *keiretsu* demonstrated high levels of vertical integration, such as Toyota. In other cases, they involved extensive horizontal linkages, such as the Mitsubishi Group, which included a hugely diverse set of company holdings: Mitsubishi Motors, Kirin Brewery, Mitsubishi Bank, Meiji Mutual Life, Mitsubishi Paper Mills, and Mitsubishi Electric.[13]

Although it was common for *Keiretsu* companies to own shares of member companies, rarely did they own majority stakes in one another. Thus, member companies were bound more by personal relationships, often-interlocking directorships, and mutual dependency than by shared ownership. Interestingly, in many ways the structure of the *keiretsu* mirrored the Japanese cultural emphasis on relationships. In their 1981 best-selling book, *The Art of Japanese Management*—written at a time when Japanese managers were warmly viewed as "artists"—Richard Pascale and Anthony Athos described the central role of interdependence in Japanese society:

> *Organizational relationships are based on interdependence ... Classically, a Japanese does not see his world in terms of separate categories (friends, relatives, subordinates), but as concentric rings of relationships, from the intimate (at the innermost) to the peripheral.*[14]

The *keiretsu* relationships and joint holdings involved facilitated vertical integration and enabled long-term commitments and mutual dependencies between large customers and suppliers and these were not necessarily the norm outside of Japan.

Consider the auto industry in the 1970s and 1980s in Japan.[15] During this period, about 70% of all parts for the big Japanese automakers were manufactured by suppliers. In the United States, the ratio was the mirror image—about 30%. Why? Because the supplier-customer relationships were completely different in the two countries. For example, in the United States, if GM wanted a new part, it would design the part, detail the specs, and put it out to bid. The lowest bidder would get the work, but the winner might change from year to year. In Japan, it happened very differently. A company like Mitsubishi would simply lay out part descriptions and desired specifications and then let a specified dedicated supplier go to all the expense and trouble of designing the part and building the part. Of course manufacturing could not begin before Mitsubishi signed off on the design and after Mitsubishi had extracted a very low price for the part from the supplier.

Why would Mitsubishi entrust so much of its value in a supplier? Why would a supplier invest so much in serving a customer and take such low price for the product and service it provided? First, the two trusted each other. Why? Part of the answer lies in the formal and informal ties that bind them together. For example, it is likely that the supplier had former Mitsubishi executives as directors and paid advisors on staff. It is also likely that the supplier would own shares of Mitsubishi Motors and Mitsubishi would own shares of the supplier. In addition, it's likely that both would be tied by their common banker—Mitsubishi Bank. Second, each party was prepared to accept short-term trade-offs for longer-term benefits. For example, the supplier accepted short-term lower prices in exchange for long-term demand stability. And the customer, Mitsubishi Motors, was prepared to accept short-term design vulnerability in exchange for the long-term cost competitiveness of outsourcing.

Obviously, Japan is not unique when it comes to tight supplier-customer relationships; they exist elsewhere in the world too. However, the common country and cultural context made them the norm in Japan. Thus, during the domestic phase of development, the supplier-customer relationships in Japan were almost exclusively between Japanese suppliers and buyers. These relationships shared a common style that, if not unique, was certainly different from many other countries.

Regulators

Much has been made of the close working relationship between business and politics in Japan in other writings,[16] and therefore here we want to highlight only the importance it played for large Japanese companies. Perhaps the role and benefit of the relationship between regulators and Japanese firms is best seen in the Ministry of International Trade and Industry (MITI). The role of MITI, established in 1949, was to formalize the cooperation of Japanese government and private industry in matters of economic development. MITI's contributions included establishing the Japan Development Bank in 1951, which provided low-cost financing to private sector companies. MITI also regulated all imports into Japan, enabling it to protect certain industries and nurture them for future growth.

In the early 1950s, MITI emphasized heavy industries as the backbone of Japan's economic development. Later, MITI would use its ability to regulate imports by targeting the importation of technology. This in turn enabled the government to refine its support for what were viewed as strategic industries—shipbuilding, steel production, electrical generation, etc. In all of these activities, MITI was aided by the coordinated efforts of the Bank of Japan which controlled the overall money supply and kept interest rates and borrowing costs low.

Especially the largest companies in Japan mastered the delicate dance of influencing government ministers and ministries. For example, when these officials retired from government service, many Japanese firms sought them out as company employees or in other cases had them thrust upon them. In either case, the common practice of "gifts from heaven" (*amakudari*) was an important aspect of mastering the regulatory aspect of the domestic business environment.

Shareholders

This uniqueness of the Japanese domestic system was extended to the dynamics of shareholders as well. In many of the largest companies, more than 25% of the total outstanding shares were controlled by other companies in their *keiretsu* family.[17] In these cases, an unwritten norm prevailed: "if you don't pressure me too much, I won't pressure you too much." In addition, most boards of directors were populated almost entirely with senior executives from *within* the company. Outside directors during the time of domestic focus for most Japanese companies were very, very rare and generally linked to *keiretsu* members. Even today, nearly all the directors on Japanese public company boards are the senior executives of the company.

In this sense, Japanese firms created mutually reinforcing, if not virtuous, cycles. By keeping foreigners out, Japanese firms could compete with each other and take care not to create domestic price wars that could hurt profits.[18] They could use exports to leverage existing capacity and lower unit costs and then use the savings to build up further capital stock capabilities at home, which along with leveraging known human capital and government relations could be directed toward producing more products for export.

SUMMARY

From this brief review, the bottom line messages are these. First, virtually all of Japan's largest companies were born and grew up in a unique and somewhat insulated Japanese environment. Second, the largest companies not only grew up in Japan but they also thrived in Japan. This was in part because they mastered six core constituencies. Between the 1950s and 1980s these constituencies were almost entirely Japanese, and being Japanese, if not unique, they were quite different from much of the rest of the world.

3

FOLLOW THE YELLOW BRICK ROAD, PART 2

In Chapter 2 we highlighted the rise of Japanese firms and their domestic orientation from the late 19th century to the mid-20th century. To keep things in perspective, remember that in 1900 Japan had a GDP per capita that ranked it #23 in the world behind countries such as Mexico, Portugal, Hungry, Chile, and Argentina. As Japanese firms modernized and mastered their domestic market, they and the entire Japanese economy grew. As they grew at home, for all the reasons we discussed in Chapter 2, Japanese firms (encouraged and helped by the government) transitioned into Stage 2 and dramatically increased their focus on exports.

THE MAKINGS OF MASTER EXPORTERS

After World War II ended, the Supreme Commander of Allied Powers (SCAP) controlled Japan. Key officials at the time believed that rapid economic development of Japan would encourage democratization while ensuring that Japan never revisited its militaristic past. Economic and political institutions were established and US government financial support flowed in. Even though SCAP control ended during the Korean War, allied military procurement and leases associated with the Korean War remained a boon to the Japanese economy through 1953.[1]

By the 1960s—a decade some refer to as the Golden Sixties—Japan, led by Prime Minister Ikeda, launched audacious plans to build infrastructure and shift the economy from a reliance on heavy industry to export-led economic development. So began the seemingly irreversible charge of Japanese companies into exporting.

Technology and quality

In order to ensure worldclass quality and world-beating costs, companies as diverse as Hitachi, Matsushita, and Canon all moved aggressively to import technology from the West, usually the United States. In many cases, the technology would be offered freely by naïve Western managers who in retrospect were all too eager to host visiting delegations of Japanese business people who were essentially industrial spies. The thinking of the Americans at the time was simple: "Who could imagine that small island purveyors of everything 'cheap' could ever be a competitive, global threat?"

With such attitudes and with Japanese companies increasing their quality, European and American producers outsourced more and more of their production to low-cost Japan, until eventually many ceased manufacturing themselves altogether. Back in Japan, production volumes continued to climb, driving unit costs ever lower. Soon the Japanese were unquestionably the lowest cost and highest quality producers on the planet across a wide variety of products.

Labor and culture

Japanese firms recognized that while having worldclass manufacturing technology was necessary, it was not sufficient. In addition, they needed to leverage the low cost and culture of their people. Culture has been described as those "beliefs and values that are widely shared in a specific society at a particular point in time."[2] It is developed over *many* years and is influenced by religion, history, geography, climate, conflict, and education, among other factors.[3] Our objective is not to exhaustively review the libraries of research on Japanese culture but rather to remind the reader of several of its key elements:

1. The Japanese tend to rely on high levels of implicit communication versus Americans, Australians, or Dutch who tend to use more explicit—say what you mean/mean what you say—approaches to communication. In Japan, there is a much higher level of responsibility on the listener to contribute to the communication process.
2. The Japanese generally emphasize collectivism much more strongly than Americans, Canadians, or the British who celebrate the individual. Collectivism pertains to an emphasis on the family or group to provide order and meaning and form the basis for decision making.

3. The Japanese tend to be more hierarchical than Americans, Swedish, or Irish are when it comes to perceived power differences in organizations. It is much less acceptable to challenge a boss in Japanese society than in the United States.
4. The Japanese generally have a much lower tolerance for uncertainty than Americans, Germans, or New Zealanders. As managers, Japanese feel heightened levels of stress when they don't have answers to questions posed by subordinates and are less prone to take major risks—either individually or on behalf of their companies.
5. The Japanese are generally more future oriented in terms of receiving rewards or gratification. Americans, in contrast, favor shorter-term payoffs and rewards that are more clearly tied to recent actions.

When you are dealing with issues of national culture, it is easy and at the same time dangerous to over-generalize. There are always outliers. Just as some Americans are happy living in a commune, it is not overly difficult to find Japanese with dyed blue hair who rail at the collectivism that is at the core of Japanese culture. Nevertheless, cultural patterns are pretty easy to see. When Americans travel, they do it alone; when Japanese travel, they do it in a group and are *led* by the ubiquitous tour guide with a flag. This image captures the essence of Japanese culture better than most. The Japanese stick together as they confront the outside world, expect a leader to take charge, and follow when asked.

It isn't that any culture is better than others; rather, it is that some cultures are *better* at producing certain kinds of behaviors than others. The same culture that promotes following tour guides with megaphones and flags is also great at encouraging people to come together as a team, hunker down in a back-room, perfect a product through endless reengineering, and drive variability out of production through mass standardization and huge production economies. The Japanese are not just great at this; they are brilliant. And this behavior is exactly what large Japanese firms needed in order to become great exporters.

It is this culture of collectivism and risk avoidance that also makes the culture so difficult to break into. Having a language that is nearly impossible for Americans or Europeans to learn and an implicit communication style, even when you know the words, do not help. The result is a very exclusive society. You are in the group—meaning you are Japanese—or you are an outsider, which includes everyone else. The exclusiveness of Japanese society contributes to a unified approach to business. New ideas are studied but not easily accepted. And this lack of acceptance of variance is central to the Japanese success as exporters. Whereas truly global organizations understand and integrate diverse value systems,[4] organizations that cannot do this will typically turn inwards, leverage cohesiveness, all of which fits well with exporting standardized products. In the 1980s when the success of Japanese firms was approaching its zenith, Jared Taylor made one of the most poignant cases about the role of culture in the success of Japanese firms.[5] He noted that the sense of uniqueness, the pervasiveness of hierarchy, group-consciousness, and conformity all contributed to cohesive work relations and commitment to the company's success. He further argued that other nations, including the United States, should not try to copy the Japanese miracle because they simply lacked the same culture as Japan and trying to copy their systems without their culture would result in failure not success.

Keeping the home market to themselves

Although at first it might not seem related, one thing that helped Japanese with their exports was not having to worry about foreigners in their home market (see Exhibit 3.1).

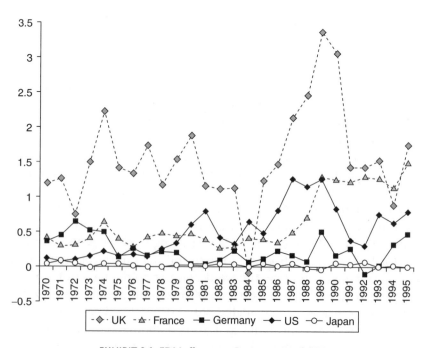

EXHIBIT 3.1 **FDI Inflow as a Percentage of GDP**
Source: United Nations World Investment Report 2008.

As an illustration of how well they kept foreigners out, consider that in 1983 an amazing 98% of all goods sold by Japanese companies were made in Japan. By 1986, this number had only dropped to 95%.[6] In addition, even as late as 1990, Japanese firms controlled 95% of the domestic Japan auto market.[7] At the same time steel production that fed the domestic automobile market was more than 90% controlled by Japanese firms.[8]

As Exhibit 3.1 shows, the level of FDI inflow as a percentage of GDP for Japan was consistently far lower than for the United States, Germany, France, and the United Kingdom. Thus, while Japan was keen on acquiring technology from foreigners, it was *not* keen on attracting foreign competitors into Japan.

Keeping foreigners out created two potential benefits. First, having a greater share of the home market helped capture economies of scale and drive down unit costs, which in turn could help keep export prices low and market share abroad high. Second, keeping foreigners out created the potential for a profit sanctuary at home. These profits could then be used to fund capital investment, process improvement, and even product development that could enhance the quality/price value proposition of Japanese exports abroad.

THE LUCK OF THE.... JAPANESE

While Japanese firms clearly pursued an intelligent path to economic development—and deserve enormous credit for it—let's not forget the importance of sheer luck in their upward march. As managers at any successful company know, luck can never be too far away.

Open trade with big markets

Fortunately for Japanese firms bent on exporting, the 1950s and 1960s were an era of growing consumerism in the United States and Europe. The world was generally at peace and markets were booming everywhere. It was difficult not to benefit from an environment where cheap exports would be warmly welcomed overseas.

In addition, the GATT (General Agreement on Tariffs and Trade) Geneva II, Dillon, Kennedy, and Tokyo rounds from January 1956 through September 1973 reduced tariffs by approximately $350 billion and reduced tariff rates by an average of 30%, which significantly benefited Japan's export oriented companies.[9]

Oil shock and Japanese automakers

For the Japanese, the oil shock of 1979 was also an external factor that helped supercharge their export machine. Specifically, it created in the largest automotive market in the world, the United States, a surge in demand for more fuel-efficient automobiles. Unable to find dependable, domestically produced automobiles, American consumers shifted to Japanese automobiles. Japanese autos were fuel-efficient because with no local source of oil, gas prices in Japan had always been high and by necessity cars there had to be frugal on fuel.

Shortly after the oil shock and its impact of pointing US consumers to Japanese fuel-efficient cars, Japanese auto firms received another blessing not of their making. In the early 1980s, Paul Volker, Chairman of the US Federal Reserve under US President Ronald Regan, lifted interest rates to draconian levels in his war on inflation. The net result was a soaring US dollar, and for Japanese automobile companies a price advantage that jumped to an estimated 40%.[10]

Dumb foreign competitors

Japanese companies were also blessed by the sheer incompetence and lack of sophistication of foreign competitors. While much has been written about the cultural barriers to doing business in Japan, lousy management on the part of American and European firms contributed to the uncontested nature of Japanese domestic markets in terms of foreign competitors. This in turn enabled Japanese firms to grow and prosper, and later develop domestic profit sanctuaries from which they could subsidize global market expansion.

Evidence from the early 1990s suggests that foreign subsidiaries operating in Japan pursued far simpler strategies to subsidiaries operating in the United States or Europe. For example, one study showed that over 75% of foreign-owned subsidiaries operating in Japan in the early 1990s were essentially miniature replicas of the parent—selling exactly the same products and services—versus only 32% of subsidiaries operating in Europe and 44% of all foreign subsidiaries operating in the United States.[11] Such approaches work great if Japanese customers are identical to those in the United States or Europe. But if not, then the foreign subsidiaries are not much of a threat.

Two brief examples illustrate the lack of sophistication, or as some would argue the stupidity of American firms operating in Japan during its boom days. First, it took decades for America's Big Three to introduce vehicles into the Japanese market that included right-hand drive steering. Not only did consumers view left-hand drives as dangerous but also awkward given the frequency of tollbooths on Japanese freeways.[12] Furthermore, American cars were viewed as large and unsuitable for the narrow streets and parking spaces in Japanese cities. In a study conducted by the US Department of Commerce in the early 1990s, only 0.2% of Japanese consumers surveyed even considered an American car in their most recent purchase decision.[13] Second, to add insult to injury, American companies failed to effectively set up their own Japanese dealer network, seeking instead to share dealers with Japanese manufacturers. Unfortunately, by the early 1990s, Japanese manufacturers owned equity positions in about one-third of their dealers; others had substantial debt with the manufacturers. What was the incentive for Japanese dealers to promote US-built cars? No wonder the American auto companies failed miserably in Japan. This failure clearly enabled the Japanese companies to generate additional profits at home and gain the upper hand in their own export efforts.

While the example of the American automobile companies is sobering, it isn't an isolated case. Companies as diverse as P&G, IBM, Avon, Wal-Mart, and General Mills all stumbled badly in establishing themselves in Japan. Like GM and Ford, they shared common problems: arrogance, an absence of good research, and half-baked commitments to getting things right. The case of General Mills is indicative of these problems. In the 1960s (earlier than most), General Mills started to turn its attention to Japan. Attracted by rising living standards, General Mills executives believed the market was ripe for its Betty Crocker brand of bake-it-at-home cakes. Most Japanese purchased cakes from bakeries and expensive pastry shops. Surely they would like to save money and show their families a little extra "love" by baking them a cake at home. Problem number one: few Japanese homes had ovens. To overcome this problem, the folks at Betty Crocker came up with the ingenious idea: use rice cookers to prepare their cakes. After all, every Japanese family owned a rice cooker. With a little tweaking of the formulation, the results looked promising. Even focus groups seemed to like the flavor and texture of the rice cooker baked cakes. But to everyone's shock, sales never materialized. What was the problem? While the cakes tasted just fine, no one told the focus groups that they were baked in a rice cooker, thus likely biasing the testing results. In Japan, the daily preparation of rice was a ritual that took on an almost sacred role in peoples' lives. Not only would baking a cake in a rice cooker "desecrate" the appliance, but it left residual tastes, destroying the flavor of the rice—at least in the minds of the Japanese. Betty Crocker has never really recovered from the blunder and today is a non-player in the bakery business in Japan.[14]

THE NET EFFECT

By 1980, the Japanese had become the world's greatest and most successful exporters and the rate of increase in the 1960s, 70s, and 80s was staggering (see Exhibit 3.2). Between 1962 and 1982, Japanese exports increased from $5 billion to $160 billion—an amazing 3,200% in current prices. From 1962 to 1982, the average annual growth in exports, year-in and year-out, was a whopping 16%, again in current prices!

During this time, exports were exploding not just in absolute values but also as a percentage of Japan's overall economy. Exhibit 3.3 compares trends in export data as a percentage of GDP for the United States versus Japan for the years 1962–1985. It shows that as a percentage of GDP, Japanese exports grew from 8.1% in 1962 to 13.9% in 1984. And this was against the backdrop of rapidly growing Japanese GDP.

But the emphasis on exports that was set in the 1960s and continued through the 1980s did not stop there. It pressed on well into the 1990s (see Exhibit 3.4). Not to put too fine a point on this extraordinary success, but we need to keep in mind that the value of the yen appreciated

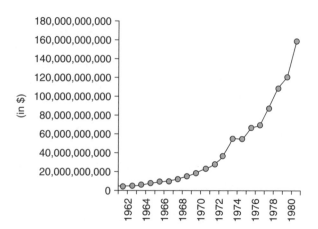

EXHIBIT 3.2 **Growth in Exports from Japan (1962–1981)**
Source: Japan Bureau of Statistics 2008.

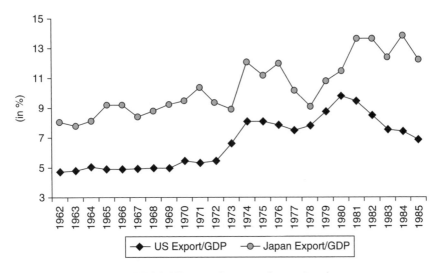

EXHIBIT 3.3 **US versus Japanese Export Levels**
Sources: Japan Bureau of Statistics 2008; US Department of Commerce, 2008.

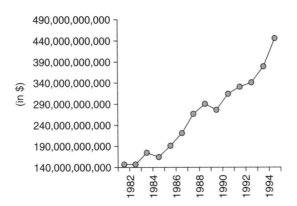

EXHIBIT 3.4 **Exports from Japan (1982–1995)**
Source: Japan Statistics Bureau, 2008.

dramatically during this period. For example, in 1982, it took 233 yen to buy one US dollar. By 1995, it only took 93 yen to buy one US dollar. This meant that Japanese goods were significantly more expensive and yet the world bought more, irrespective of whether exports were measured in US dollars or Japanese yen.

By the late 1980s, Japanese factories were stamping out and assembling products that came to dominate a huge range of industries throughout the developed world. The Japanese beat the British in the motorcycle business, eclipsed the Germans and Americans in automobile production, demolished the Swiss in watches and optical equipment, and overcame the dominance of the Americans in steel. What followed from this low cost, high quality position was *power* and with it, the ability to introduce their own brands for which they could now begin to command premium prices. Before long, they were unassailable.

THE CRAZY 1980s

During the 1980s, Japanese companies took off and became giants in size and esteem. The covers of business publications including *Fortune* magazine and *Business Week* regularly lauded the successes of Japanese companies. For *Time* magazine, the cover of its March 30, 1981 edition put it best: "How Japan Does It: The World's Toughest Competitor." Five years later, *The Economist*'s October 25, 1986 cover featured the picture of a giant samurai holding a pint-sized Uncle Sam doll with the caption "Now I'm Richer than you." Not to be outdone, the *Harvard Business Review,* during one five-year period in the mid-1980s, included no less than 36 different articles either praising the Japanese or fretting about the power of Japanese companies. Articles with titles like "Demystifying Japanese Management Practices"[15] or "Power without Purpose: The Crisis of Japanese Global Financial Dominance"[16] were common.

The 1980s was also known as a decade when Japanese companies flexed their muscles. It was a decade during which the sun never seemed to set on Japan Inc. The combination of a booming economy and cheap money led to what we now know as the infamous Japanese real estate bubble. Prices in the Ginza district peaked in 1989, with the best properties demanding nearly $140,000 sq/foot. Other areas of Tokyo were nearly as pricey. At one point, it was widely reported that the Imperial Palace in Tokyo (about 208 acres) was worth more than the entire state of California (which on its own, was the 7th largest economy in the world at the time). Not only did the roaring 1980s impact property prices, but Japanese business people, flush with cash, also drove up the price of vacation homes in Hawaii and golf club memberships at home. At its peak, it was estimated that the total market value of golf club memberships in Japan was about $200 billion,[17] exceeding the total GDPs of the countries of Greece, Denmark, and Israel. Buoyed by soaring prices, Japanese development companies went on buying binges around the world where every building looked cheap. Their efforts reached a zenith in 1989 when Mitsubishi Estate, the real estate arm of Mitsubishi Group, announced it would pay $846 million in cash for a 51% stake in Rockefeller Center. The deal shocked Americans and made the front pages of virtually every newspaper in the country: "If they can pay this much for half of Rockefeller Center, nothing is safe."

By the late 1980s, the Tokyo Stock Exchange finally surpassed the NYSE to become the world's largest in terms of market capitalization. The Osaka exchange became the world's third largest, bumping the LSE to the number four position.[18] Of the world's ten largest banks in 1989, nine were based in Japan. Even the Japanese Postal Savings System, a quasi-state controlled bank, with assets in 1989 approaching $1 trillion, was larger than the top 12 US banks combined.[19]

SUMMARY

Japan as a country and its largest companies started the modern domestic stage of development toward the end of the 19th century with the *Meiji* Restoration. That domestic development stage continued for another 60 years. After World War II, the Japanese economy in general and Japan's largest firms in particular refocused on the domestic market and then in the 1960s, 70s, and 80s mastered exports. In 1962, Japanese firms had nominal exports of just $4.9 billion. By 1985, that had increased to over $165 billion—a 33-fold increase! By 1995, even off this much higher base, exports more than doubled to $447 billion. To put this into perspective, consider that in 1995 Japanese exports *alone* were greater than the entire GDP of India, a country with 10 times Japan's population. Leveraging its mastery of its home market, including demanding Japanese customers, Japanese firms utilized their own as well as the technology of others, improved quality, captured economies of scale, and lowered unit costs to near perfection. However, as we will examine in the next chapter, what helps you at home and with exports is not what is required to succeed as you transition into the regional and global stages of development.

4

A BRAVE NEW WORLD

In Chapters 2 and 3, we painted a reasonable but somewhat simplified picture of the path to borderless globalization and discussed the success of Japanese companies in the first two stages of our model—domestic focus and exports. We now can dive deeper into the keys to making the leap from export to the regional and from regional to the global stages. This in turn sets the stage for why we believe Japanese firms will continue to struggle in a global future.

REGIONAL STAGE OF DEVELOPMENT AND GROWTH

As we mentioned briefly in Chapter 2, growth only through exports typically reaches a limit because the segment of customers who want products and services adapted to their local needs is usually larger than the segment that is happy to accept the standardized product exported to them. However, for the vast majority of companies who want to truly understand and deliver what their international customers want, they have to move out of the home country and build up capabilities overseas. In fact, expanding the geographic footprint of the firm is a natural move for companies eager to grow.

This simple fact is critical because although people are fond of saying, "The world is getting smaller," the world is actually getting bigger. As strange as it may seem, the fact is that the world today is bigger than it was in 1960—not geographically, but in terms of the number and accessibility of countries and territories. Quite literally, the number of countries and territories has expanded by about 25% over the past 40 years. Much of this came after 1989 with the break up of the former Soviet Union. In addition, if you looked around the world at places such as China, Vietnam, Romania, Cambodia, the Czech Republic, Libya, and Russia, you would quickly realize that these countries are far more accessible than they were 20 years ago. For example, just think about the size of foreign direct investment flowing into China in 1989. It was about $3 billion. Doing business there was not easy and not for the fainthearted. Twenty years later, it's amazing to see the number of foreign companies doing business in China and the size of foreign direct investment going into the country. For example, in 1989, KFC had a grand total of 3 stores in China; in 2008, it operated 2,500 stores. In 2008 alone, FDI into China exceeded $80 billion or greater than the total GDP of Vietnam.

So in practical "business growth" terms, the world has expanded. As a consequence, companies can grow their business by expanding into geographies in which they did not have a presence before. They can also expand the size of their business in countries where their previous presence was restricted. This is essential for regional expansion and is the *sin qua non* of borderless global competition and growth.

Japanese firms' lagging geographic expansion

It is easy to think that because you can go to almost any place in the world today and see Japanese brands such as Sony, Panasonic, and Canon that they expanded and grew geographically just fine. Sadly, the facts don't bear this out. In saying this, we don't intend to create the impression that Japanese firms did not invest in building up capacity and capabilities outside Japan. They did. The problem was that they did it at relatively lower levels than the companies from other economic powerhouse countries did; and they did it in ways that kept them from fully tapping into local, regional, and global human capital capabilities outside Japan.

Tracking FDI flows

The most direct evidence of the comparatively low levels of the geographic expansion of Japanese MNCs is in the level of foreign direct investment outflows. However, you cannot look just at absolute outflows of FDI because larger countries will of course in general have larger FDI outflows. Rather, in order to compare countries of different economic size, you need to look at the ratio of FDI relative to the country's economic size.

Exhibit 4.1 shows the FDI outflows by country as a percentage of each country's GDP. As this chart illustrates, Japan has been increasing

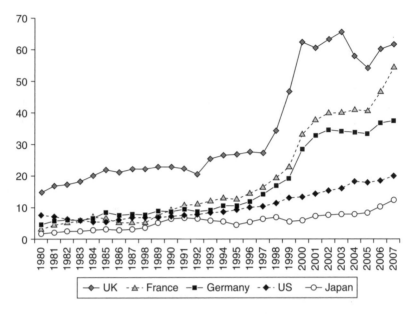

EXHIBIT 4.1 **FDI Outflows by Country as a Percentage of GDP**
Source: UNCTAD World Investment Report 2008.

both the total size of FDI outflows and the proportion of those outflows relative to GDP. However, Japan's relative increase of FDI outflows as a percentage of GDP compared to other key countries has
lost ground over time. Exhibit 4.1 clearly shows that from 1980 to
1991, Japan's investment in foreign countries as a percentage of its
GDP tracked similarly to that of the United States, Germany, and
France. However, from the early 1990s onward they diverge. While
Japan's relative FDI ratio declined through 1995, the same ratios for
the United Kingdom, United States, Germany, and France increased.
This gap continued until 2006 and 2007 when Japan narrowed the
gap with the United States and Germany but not with France and the
United Kingdom. In part, it is this relatively lower level of FDI as a per-
centage of Japan's GDP in relation to that of the United States, United
Kingdom, Germany, and France that *helps* explain why the number
of Japanese companies in the United Nation's Top 100 Transnational
Companies declined by 50%. Fundamentally, Japanese companies
were trying to catch up to a train that was way down the track and
accelerating faster than they were running after it.

A slightly more complicated but more representative way to look
at the behavior of Japanese companies is to examine how much of
their focus and money were going into exports relative to how much

were going into FDI outflows. Exhibit 4.2 captures this for Japan and provides the United States as a point of comparison. As the chart indicates, at Japan's export peak in the 1980s, it was exporting over $6 worth of product for every $1 it was investing abroad. Keep in mind that this means Japanese companies were having to invest in physical and human capital capabilities *in Japan* in order to achieve this level of export output. The ratio of exports to FDI outflow declined significantly for Japanese companies until leveling off at about $1.5 in exports for every $1 invested abroad. However, over the same period, the United States went from a ratio of $1.2 in exports for every $1 in FDI to a ratio of $0.41 in exports for every $1 in FDI.

In other words, in 2007, Japanese firms were still placing 3 times as much emphasis on exports relative to FDI outflows as were US firms. As we discussed in the previous chapter, the problem with this is that progress out of domestic and export stages on the path to globalization requires significant investment in and building up of physical and human capital capabilities outside one's home country—regardless of how large that home economy is. Japanese companies were simply not doing this at a fast enough rate. This inhibited them from fully capturing the growth benefits of geographic expansion from 1995 until now. Again, they were falling behind.

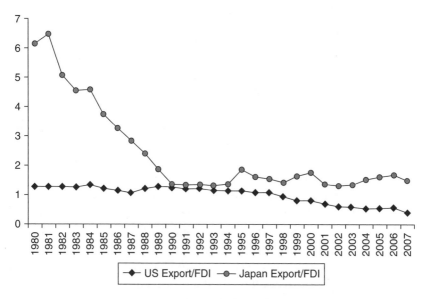

EXHIBIT 4.2 **Ratio of Exports to FDI**
Source: UNCTAD World Investment Report 2008.

This relatively low rate of capability build-up outside Japan became increasingly important because the countries with the highest growth rates from 1995 onward were also outside Japan. As we said, the problem was not that Japanese companies were blind to the need to move out of the domestic and export stages of development; rather the problem was that they were somewhat slow to act on that recognition and were simply not aggressive enough in their reaction. As a consequence, Japanese companies were simply not running fast enough to catch up to a train that was far ahead of them and that was accelerating away faster than they were running after it.

The *Fortune Global 500* rankings

We can see these same basic patterns again and again as we look closer at the Japanese companies in the *Fortune Global 500* list in 1995 and in 2008 (see Exhibit 4.3). As we can see from Exhibit 4.3, in 1995, Daiei was #73 on the list and Ito-Yokado was #90, but by 2008 both had dropped out of the *Fortune Global 500*. Not only were these two firms among the 100 largest in the world in 1995 but they were also among the largest retailers in all of Japan in 1995. Unfortunately, both were largely focused on the Japanese domestic market in 1995 and remained so over the next 17 years.

This inability to transition from domestic focus to a more regional or global focus lost them their place among the global firms in the world. We can contrast these two Japanese firms to two similar firms in Europe that did move along the path to globalization over this same period. For example, in 1995, Germany's Metro was not large enough to even make the Global 500 list but by 2008 was #56 on the list and had nearly 20% of its sales from outside Germany. In 1995, Carrefour was #95 on the list and by 2008 was ranked #33 with more than half its sales outside of France.

As we can see from Exhibit 4.3, the decline of top Japanese firms was dramatic. While 2 of the 25 firms fell off the list between 1995 and 2008, of the remaining 23 firms 21 dropped in ranking, with the average decline of 129 positions! The largest declines were among the five large trading firms (Mitsubishi, Mitsui, Itochu, Sumitomo, and Marubeni). These firms at the time focused heavily on import and export trade and not on investing in and building up capabilities in foreign markets. Unfortunately, they did not adjust their focus outside Japan enough and declined in ranking by an average of 202 positions over the next 17 years.

EXHIBIT 4.3 **Top 25** *Fortune Global 500* Japanese Firms' Fate

Company	1995 Global ranking	2008 Global ranking	Change
Mitsubishi	1	130	−129
Mitsui	2	140	−138
Itochu	3	322	−319
Sumitomo	5	236	−231
Marubeni	6	201	−195
Toyota	8	5	+3
Hitachi	13	48	−35
Nippon Life Insurance	14	115	−101
NTT	15	54	−39
Matsushita Electric	19	210	−191
Nissan Motor	23	50	−27
Dai-Ichi Mutual Life Insurance	26	180	−154
Toshiba	32	91	−59
Tokyo Electric Power	33	146	−113
Sumitomo Life Insurance	36	269	−233
Sony	40	75	−35
NEC	45	174	−129
Honda Motor	46	40	+6
Fujitsu	54	149	−95
Meiji Life Insurance	57	242	−185
Mitsubishi Motors	62	350	−288
Daiei	73	Off the List	−
Mitsubishi Heavy Industries	85	285	−200
Nippon Steel	88	165	−77
Ito-Yokado	90	Off the List	−

Source: *Fortune Global 500* list 1995, 2008.

The other big decliners included four insurance companies. These four companies experienced an average decline of 168 positions between 1995 and 2008. In 1995, these firms also focused primarily on their domestic business and remained so over the next nearly two decades. In contrast, ING, which at #92 in 1995, was ranked lower than all the Japanese insurance companies (Nippon Life Insurance #14, Dai-Ichi Mutual Life Insurance #26, Sumitomo Life Insurance #36, and Meiji Life Insurance #57), moved aggressively out of its domestic focus and expanded its geographic and portfolio coverage over the next 17 years, rising to #13 on the list by 2008. By 2008, ING was getting 79% of its revenue from outside the Netherlands.

This pattern of insufficient focus outside Japan affected the other Japanese firms on the list as well and caused a fall in their rankings. Of the seven Japanese firms that declined by 75 positions or more between 1995 and 2008, on average only 32% of their revenue came from outside Japan by 2008. In contrast, of the five companies that declined by less than 75 points over this period, on average they received over 55% of their revenues from outside Japan by 2008.

Finally, only two Japanese firms improved their ranking over this period—Honda and Toyota. Both firms made significant investments to build up physical and human capital capabilities outside Japan between 1995 and 2008. In Honda's case, in 2008, approximately 86% of their auto sales and 94% of their motorcycles sales came from outside Japan.[1] A total of 77% of its production employees were located outside Japan. By 2008, over 65% of Toyota's revenue came from outside Japan;[2] still, a full 60% of its production was still coming from *inside* Japan. Not bad by Japanese norms, but it may not be enough. Why? First, Toyota's financial situation deteriorated at an unprecedented pace in the 2008–2009 recession. Part of their problem was slow decision making, over-reliance on Japan for product ideas, and relatively lower levels of FDI than many of its European competitors. Nowhere is this better seen than in China—the only market that was still growing during the 2008–2009 recession. In the first quarter of 2009, GM's sales in China grew by 17%; Toyota's fell by 17%. Why? First, Toyota suffered from low capacity. But their Japan-centric decision making and shortage of strong Chinese decision makers also resulted in their failure to anticipate and then quickly react to the changing demand patterns in China. The big market opportunities in China were actually emerging outside the large coastal cities. And here, customers were demanding small, cheap cars. GM, with a huge local presence picked up on this early; Toyota, did not.[3]

SUMMARY OF THE CHALLENGES OF A REGIONAL APPROACH

The fundamental problem of low FDI outflows relative to GDP or exports is that it keeps your eye focused on domestic-based capabilities and prevents you from diving into a deeper understanding of foreign customers, competitors, employees, partners, and stakeholders. Understanding these core constituencies in foreign markets is essential to effective geographic expansion, which is a critical driver of growth in the regional stage of development. If you are not present in the foreign market, you have a hard time understanding local customers—what they want and how their needs are different from customers in your home market. If you can't deeply understand the local customers, you can't adjust or design products that best suit their needs. And, if your eye is on the domestic production base for both your domestic market and exports, you can't fully understand or develop the foreign leaders and employees that you have or need—those that could help you understand and serve foreign customers.

There are many examples of companies that suffered mightily when they entered foreign markets without first understanding the local customers and norms. In some cases, these misunderstandings were literally a function of not understanding the local language well enough. To be fair, this is a problem for all companies, not just the Japanese, as illustrated in the examples below:

- The Japanese company **Matsushita Electric** was promoting a new Japanese PC for internet users and licensed cartoon character Woody Woodpecker. The ads for the new product featured the following slogan: "Touch Woody—The Internet Pecker." Once someone explained how this might be taken, Panasonic pulled the plug on the ad.
- The Swedish furniture giant **IKEA** somehow agreed upon the name "FARTFULL" for one of its new desks.
- In Germany, "Irish Mist" (an alcoholic drink), "Mist Stick" (a curling iron from Clairol), and "Silver Mist" (Rolls Royce car) all flopped because "mist" in German means dung/manure.
- **Umbro** the UK sports manufacturer had to withdraw its new trainers (sneakers) called the Zyklon because it was the name of the gas used by the Nazi regime to murder millions of Jews in concentration camps.
- **Honda** introduced their new car "Fitta" into Nordic countries in 2001 but soon changed the name to "Honda Jazz" after learning that "fitta" was an old word used in vulgar language to refer to a woman's genitals in Swedish, Norwegian, and Danish.

Beyond the momentum effect of the 35 years of success at home and with exports that kept Japanese MNCs' eyes at home instead of abroad, what else contributed to their difficulty in transitioning to and moving more deeply into the regional stage? We have identified three separate factors that we examine in detail in the next three chapters. However, before that, we need to also take a closer look at the global stage of development and what is required for growth in that stage.

Global stage of development and growth

As firms move more deeply into the regional stage of development, they adapt and adjust to different markets. Ironically, the adjustments that are truly necessary and which serve as positive factors of growth at the regional stage can become inhibitors of growth in the global stage. As we discussed earlier, as companies push into more and more countries and make more and more local adjustments, the aggregate cost of those adjustments start to add up. For example, at its peak, Warner Lambert had 63 different formulations of "Halls" that ranged from positioning Halls as a cough drop in North American to positioning it as a hard candy in Brazil, and everything in between. Therefore, as we discussed in Chapter 2, one of the fundamental challenges in the global stage of development is to determine (1) what should be globally integrated or standardized, (2) what should be localized, and (3) what should be a blend and how much of a blend of each. Without meeting this challenge, the aggregate costs of just pure localization can skyrocket.

In addition, companies at the global stage of development have an additional challenge—how can they continue to grow the top line? By the time companies get to the global stage of development, they are not only already present in most countries but their level of investment in all those foreign countries is also relatively high. In fact, that investment is principally how they got deep into the regional stage of development. By this point, growth through more geographic expansion starts to run out of gas. Don't misunderstand us; it is not the case that geographic expansion is not important even at the global stage but its relative importance as a growth driver diminishes. What companies need is to add another engine of growth. Companies need to not just move *into* new countries but also expand market share in the geographies in which they are already present.

Role of innovation in global growth

Part of the reason why market share expansion is critical is because, while developing markets are growing faster, the developed markets in which most MNCs already operate are significantly larger. In fact, the developed markets of North America, Western Europe, and Japan represent more than 67% of the world's total GDP. Furthermore, the demand in developing countries is often misaligned with the offerings of many Western companies. For example, in many developing countries hawker stalls sell cheap street food at prices and in settings that can't or wouldn't be matched by the likes of KFC or McDonalds.

They also frequently distribute drinks and sauces in small plastic bags sealed with cheap rubber bands, cutting into the potential market for Western bottlers. These differences are real and cut into the actual potential of these markets *today* for companies from the developed world. Therefore, as companies move from export to regional and global stages of development, companies are almost forced to focus on growth in developed markets. Developed markets are called so because they are *developed*. As a consequence, if you want to grow in such markets you must innovate; you have to come up with new products, new processes, and new business models that grow the market for you.

You can think of this sort of innovation as moving you into new competitive space. In 1994, a pair of authors (Hamel and Prahalad) called this domain "whitespace."[4] About 10 years later, a different pair of authors (Kim and Mauborgne) labeled it "blue ocean."[5] Whatever the label, the basic notion is that innovation that puts you in less rather than more contested space leads to higher growth and is more profitable.

While product and service innovations that move you into less contested space are good and necessary, they are both difficult and somewhat unpredictable and therefore, typically not sufficient. Process innovation that creates greater speed to market, enhanced efficiency, and other benefits is also typically necessary. Process innovations that lower costs and enhance margins can in one sense be the source of funding for whitespace or blue ocean product innovation expeditions.

Finally, innovations that rewrite or dramatically alter the business model as we have seen through companies like Amazon.com, Apple iTunes, or Google are also keys to retaining the ability to grow in large, developed markets. Unfortunately for incumbents, coming up with and embracing innovative business models may be the most difficult task of all because they often have throw out, sell off, or cannibalize legacy models upon which their success was historically built. This is in part why most new business model innovations come from new companies.

Obviously, innovations that help you in developed markets typically don't hurt you in developing markets. In this sense, product, process, or business model innovation can help you with both geographic and market expansion. But depending on the demand patterns in developing markets, the benefits of these models may take longer to realize.

The drivers of innovation

If customers in developed markets are going to come to you instead of your competitors, you need something that is better and different from others. Innovation is obviously at the heart of any differentiation in terms of product, service, process, or business model. So what drives innovation? Entire books could be and have been written on the keys to innovation, so there is no way we want to even pretend to present a comprehensive review here. Rather, we want to take just a bit of time and space to highlight the key drivers of innovation in order to come back to them in the next chapter with a specific look at how they relate to the challenge of Japanese firms in the global future.

One of the first drivers of innovation in business is diversity.[6] If you put ten people in a room who have exactly the same view of the world, how can they come up with something new, different, and innovative? Innovation requires people with different perspectives, points of view, expertise, experience, education, etc. coming together and even colliding in order to generate the sparks that illuminate new insight and ideas. This turns out to be the case even for lone, individual geniuses. Those inventors with the most consistent histories of innovation tend to gain their sparks of new insight by looking at a problem from different angles or bringing together in their own mind different perspectives.[7]

However, the research and practice is clear that simply throwing a bunch of different people, perspectives, background, cultures, languages, education, personalities, etc. into a room and mixing them around will not automatically result in innovation. In fact, research has shown that on average a homogeneous group will outperform a diverse group that is just thrown together.[8] Why? Because the differences that are in fact critical to sparking innovation are also quite robust at sparking conflicts, disagreements, mistrust, and other dysfunctional dynamics that hurt group performance.

However, *if* the conflicts, disagreements, etc. that the diversity sparks are well managed, then diverse groups actually outperform more homogeneous groups in terms of innovation. Thus, the second thing we know about the key drivers of innovation is that effective leadership of the innovators is critical to success.

These leaders need a combination of skills. First, they need significant interpersonal and group management skills in areas such as drawing out contributions and thoughts and managing conflicts. Second, they must be able to periodically remind and keep the group on task. This is because creativity left undirected toward an objective can quickly and easily spin into chaos. Third, the leaders of innovative groups need a high degree of self-awareness in terms of their own strengths, weaknesses, biases, and tendencies. Why does self-awareness matter? It matters because regardless of how open to others one desires to be, it is impossible to completely escape one's own history and biases. No one is a blank sheet of paper. Everyone comes with cultural, educational, gender, experience, and other "baggage" that shapes how one naturally sees and interprets the world. In addition, virtually no one has the capacity to look at a problem or even a proposed solution from every possible angle. Just think about it. If you were trying to come up with the next innovation that would put the iPod on the antique shelf, whom do you know (including yourself) who has had the full training in all relevant hardware expertise, software capabilities, all germane music culture knowledge, all pertinent experiences, all applicable insights, all appropriate perspectives to meet that innovation challenge? No one. As a consequence, the leader of innovation needs to not only manage the relational and task dynamics of the group but also monitor, regulate, and augment his or her own capabilities in the overall process.

The research on what leads to the development of such leaders of innovation is still a bit new and thin, but it seems that to some extent what is required for effective leadership of innovation is innate and ties back to the characteristic of curiosity, including toward self-insight, that we discussed before.[9] However, like a gifted athlete or musician, while innate talent or aptitude is necessary, it doesn't necessarily or automatically translate into performance. You may have a natural gift for jumping high but that doesn't mean you will automatically win the Olympic gold medal in the high jump. It takes some dedicated training, practice, and development. The same is true for an effective leader of innovation; you may have some innate curiosity or interpersonal skills, but without some experience, training, and coaching, you are unlikely to walk away with any innovation performance records.

Fundamental requirements for global success

From this discussion, we can distill some fundamental requirements for success in the global world, both today and in the future. First, transitioning into the regional stage necessarily requires geographic expansion. This in turn necessitates dealing effectively with customer, competitor, employee, partner, regulator, and stakeholder differences across cultures and countries. Second, transitioning to a borderless, global stage requires finding the optimal configuration of global integration and local responsiveness and producing the product, process, and/or business model innovation needed to deliver additional growth beyond geographic expansion.

The common "red thread" through it all is differences. If you are not open to and interested in differences in customers, employees, markets, new products, business models, etc. you simply have no hope of transitioning into, let alone succeeding at, the regional and global stages of development. Not only managing but also embracing differences is critical to global success.

In a separate study of global leaders we did in conjunction with another colleague a few years back, this interest in differences (we called it inquisitiveness) turned out to be one of the defining and differentiating characteristics of effective global leaders.[10] In our interviews of over 130 executives around the world, it became quite easy to identify these individuals. All you needed to do was to ask them to talk through about a month's worth of schedule. What all the global executives had in common were conference calls, emails, meetings, and trips to and with various parts of the world. What quickly differentiated the more effective from the less effective was whether all the differences in culture, regulations, customer preferences, etc. brought about by these global activities were energizing or draining. For those who had low levels of general curiosity in new, different, novel things, the nature of global business just drained them. For those who were full of inquisitiveness, global business was invigorating.

While interest in and comfort with differences is a necessary condition for effective global leadership as well as the strategy they support, it is not sufficient. You also need to make it all work. You need to be able to determine which aspects of the business to globally integrate and standardize and which ones to locally adapt and differentiate. Both research and practice clearly indicate that this takes experience. You need experience with differences, diversity, conflict, and the like. As you gain this experience you move up the experience curve going from lower to higher proficiency in dealing with diversity.

Only through selecting for aptitude, building up experience, and translating these two building blocks into actual capability can you succeed in moving out of the domestic and export stages of development and into the regional stage and beyond it into the borderless global stage.

5

CURVE BALL

In the previous chapter we documented the relative lack of FDI out-flow investments of Japanese MNCs and discussed how this kept them from moving fully into the regional stage of development. As we saw, it is pretty difficult to jump into the global stage of development without a regional stopover. In this chapter we will deal in detail with two factors that inhibited the transition of Japanese MNCs out of the export stage and into the regional and global stages. The two factors are the early performance of Japanese companies abroad and the ability of Japanese executives to tolerate risk.

PERFORMANCE ABROAD AND TOLERANCE FOR RISK

In order to appreciate the role of early performance abroad and tolerance for risk, we have to understand an important dynamic in the transition from the domestic to exporting stage versus from the exporting to the regional stage. While exporting is not the same as competing at home, both focus on *leveraging* "at-home" capabilities. In contrast, moving from the exporting to the regional stage requires a change in focus—from *leveraging* "at-home" capabilities to *developing* "foreign" capabilities. Simplified, moving from the domestic to export stage of development requires moving up the existing learning curve while moving from the exporting to the regional stage requires moving on to a new learning curve.

It is important to restate that Japanese firms did move on to this new learning curve and did make investments outside Japan, but their movement onto and up this new learning curve and the associated investments came later and in relatively smaller amounts than their competitors in Europe and the United States. In order to understand why this was the case, we need to ask, "Why were Japanese foreign investments relatively small and slow?"

When people or companies do venture out and try new things, the learning process has a general pattern to it, typically called an experience or learning curve. These curves are characterized by a pattern in which you put in significant time and energy (investments) early on only to have very little to show for it (returns). This tends to be a natural inhibitor for trying out new things.

For example, if you take up learning a new language such as Greek, or new sport such as golf, or new musical instrument such as the violin, you will not be good at it straight away. It will take you time, energy, practice, and probably money for instruction, coaching, etc. before you start to see even a little progress. Actual achievement or progress in the early stage of any learning curve is modest. In fact, in virtually all cases, it can almost seem like you are going backward. It seems this way because the "effort-outcome" ratio on the new learning curve is much worse compared to the one on the old learning curve that you have mastered. Not only this, but often on the new learning curve you are going backward because you end up paying what we refer to as a "change penalty." A change penalty happens when in doing the new thing actual outcomes get worse.

A simple example of this is Tiger Woods. Despite his recent bad press, it is important to remember not only his golfing prowess but also his path to golfing greatness. Twice in his career up through 2008, Tiger went out and got a coach and changed his swing. In both cases, he changed his swing when wins, top 10 finishes, and earnings from his finishes were all on the upswing—not when his performance was going down. Nevertheless, after he changed his swing, his performance in terms of PGA wins and Major wins got worse before improving and finally surpassing his previous level of performance (see Exhibit 5.1). In fact, the change penalty was so visible, people in general and the media in particular questioned why he would want to alter his swing when things were going so well for him. Tiger fought through the change penalty and eventually his overall performance improved, but many individuals and companies do not persevere. As a consequence, for most individuals and companies, the worse they are at the new activity and the longer it takes to improve, the higher the likelihood that the individual or company will give up and go back to what they were doing before.

In addition, tolerance for risk (or conversely preference for certainty) affects how individuals or collections of individuals react to the early stages of learning curves. Specifically, the lower your tolerance for risk (or the conversely the higher your need for certainty relative to

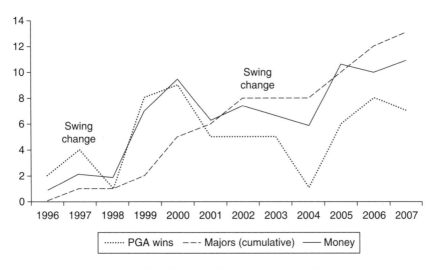

EXHIBIT 5.1 **Tiger's Swing Change Penalty and Reward**
Source: www.PGA.com.

the payoff for your efforts), the less likely you will continue or move aggressively forward in the early stages of a learning curve.[1]

At this point you might ask, "Yes, I know this. This is common sense. But what does this have to do with Japanese firms expanding or not expanding outside of Japan?" Great question to which there is a two-part answer. The first part of the answer looks at how well or poorly Japanese firms fared in their overseas expansions and the second looks at their general propensity for risk.

Japanese overseas performance

As we pointed out in Chapter 4, between 1982 and 1990, Japanese firms did make important changes and did increase their emphasis on FDI relative to their emphasis on exports. A key question is, "what were the returns on those early investments abroad?" While it is difficult to precisely calculate the return on those investments, the Japanese government's Bureau of Statistics does provide some figures that give us certain insights. Beginning in 1983, the government has reported the aggregate sales and profits of all Japanese overseas subsidiaries. As a consequence, Exhibit 5.2 provides the return on sales for Japanese overseas subsidiaries from 1983 through 2002 (the most recent year of reported data at the time of this book's printing).

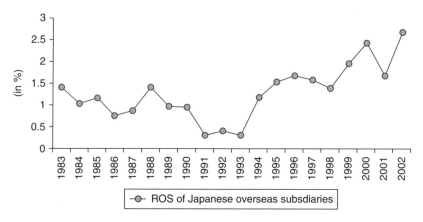

EXHIBIT 5.2 **Return on Sales of Japanese Overseas Subsidiaries**
Source: Japan Bureau of Statistics 2008.

As the chart shows, between 1983 and 1993 (the period in which Japanese firms made the relative shift toward greater FDI) ROS of Japanese overseas affiliates averaged only 0.87%. Sadly, less than 1% ROS is not great by almost any standard. As a consequence, this decade of poor return on FDI investments would be discouraging for any company. For the next decade, ROS for Japanese overseas subsidiaries improved and averaged 1.79%—better but still not great.

While both 0.87% and 1.79% ROS figures do not seem great, we can make some concrete comparisons. However, because the Japanese government does not publish company-specific results, we need to look at an alternative source of data for comparison. One that we have used all along in this book is the *Fortune Global 500* list, and so we will use it again here (see Exhibit 5.3).

In Exhibit 5.3 we see the overall ROS of all the Japanese, US, German, French, and British firms in the *Fortune Global 500* list, beginning with the first global list in 1995 and then at five-year increments but also including 2008. Generally, the overall ROS for Japanese firms has exceeded what they have obtained from their overseas operations. This is true even for Japanese firm's worst year in 1995 when the overall ROS was pulled down primarily by large losses from Japan's biggest banks. Thus, it seems likely that Japanese firms tended to move less aggressively out of the domestic and export stages and into the regionalization and globalization stages in part because of their less-than-ideal performance in these early overseas experiences.

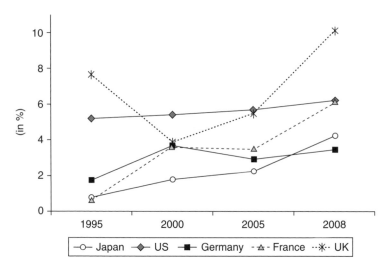

EXHIBIT 5.3 **Return on Sales by Country of Origin**
Source: *Fortune Global 500* list 1995, 2000, 2005, 2008.

Tolerance for risk

Many studies have examined national levels of risk tolerance and have systematically and consistently concluded that there are significant differences across countries. Geert Hostede conducted arguably the largest comparison study, which included over 100,000 individuals from 40 different countries.[2] In his landmark work, he found that on average Japanese were some of the most risk-averse people in the world. On average the Japanese were more than twice as risk-averse as the Americans and British, 40% more risk-averse as Germans, and 7% more risk-averse as the French. While the precise differences in tolerance for risk in this or any other study do not perfectly predict Japanese companies' favoring what is known and familiar (that is, the domestic market and exporting from their home market) versus what is foreign and unfamiliar, an important correlation is evident between the higher than average avoidance of uncertainty and the relatively low focus on foreign direct investment by Japanese firms.

In summary, doing well at home in a market that was well understood and provided less risk contributed to Japanese firms' tendency to linger in the domestic and export phases of globalization. While no doubt Japanese decision makers intellectually recognized the need to push into the more advanced stages of globalization, their companies' poor initial performance overseas combined with their lower personal tolerances for risk and higher desire for certainty arguably held them back from going as far or as fast as companies in the United States, United Kingdom, Germany, or France. In addition, in the back of Japanese executives' minds, it is quite possible (and based on our experience likely) that the long history of domestic and export success exerted a constant and compelling gravitation pull, drawing them back toward a learning curve that they had already mastered and pulling them away from a more global focus with its inherent risks and uncertainties. While this is impossible to prove, keep in mind that from 1990 to 1994 the Export/FDI ratio averaged an all time low 1.3, but from 1995 onward through 2007 it shifted back toward favoring exports over FDI and the ratio increased 23% to 1.6.

THE DEATH OF JOE ISUZU

One of the best illustrations of the challenges Japanese companies face in breaking the exporting barrier is found in the history of Isuzu Motors. The Tokyo-based company traces its origins to 1916, when Tokyo Ishikawajima Shipbuilding and Engineering got together with Tokyo Gas and Electric Industrial Company to build cars.[3] In 1922, the company produced its first automobile, the A-9, followed by the company's first truck in 1924. After World War II, Isuzu grew in Japan largely on the back of its truck sales. Its trucks were popular in Japan for their rugged durability and played a major role in building the country's infrastructure.

In an effort to improve its car technology, Isuzu signed a technical agreement with UK-based Rootes. Based on this imported technology, Isuzu introduced the Hilman Minx automobile in 1953. In the 1960s, they introduced other passenger cars for the Japanese domestic market, including the Florian, Bettett, and 117 Coupe. They also launched several new truck designs.[4]

Ever eager to expand internationally, Isuzu began looking for options and in 1971 established a partnership agreement with General Motors. The next year, it exported what Chevrolet branded the "LUV" from Japan. Two years later, with production help from GM, it introduced the Gemini in Japan and exported the car to the United States branded as Buick's Opel. Following patterns set by the likes of Matsushita and Hitachi, which started as OEM exporters before launching their own brands, Isuzu was finally successful at introducing its own Isuzu-branded car in 1981—the Isuzu "P'uP." In 1983, it introduced the

"Trooper" SUV and together both vehicles began to capture the public's attention.

In what was billed a stroke of advertising genius, in 1986 Isuzu introduced pitchman "Joe Isuzu" to the American market. Appearing on television, the ads reached their zenith in 1987 when they appeared on Super Bowl XXI. Joe Isuzu was the pure American invention of the Madison Avenue ad agency Della Femina, Travisano, and Partners. He became famous for his outlandish lies including "you have my word on it," and "it has more seats in it than the Astrodome."

Worried about working too closely with its American partner, in 1987 Isuzu entered into a joint venture (JV) with Fuji Heavy Industries, parent company of Subaru. Together, they built an assembly plant in Lafayette, Indiana. The JV created the Isuzu Rodeo and the Isuzu Pickup.

In another move, the company signed a vehicle exchange agreement with another Japanese company, Honda. In exchange for offering Honda the Isuzu Rodeo (which was sold as the Honda Passport) and the Isuzu Trooper (sold as the Acura SLX), Honda provided its Odyssey minivan to Isuzu, which Isuzu re-branded as the Oasis.

During the 1990s, Isuzu enjoyed relatively healthy car sales in the United States. Its US sales peaked in 1996, largely due to the success of its Trooper SUV. In 1999, GM increased its ownership of Isuzu to 49%, which gave it effective control of the company. It soon appointed an American executive to head up Isuzu's North American operations. One of the executive's first moves: bring back Joe Isuzu to offset sliding sales of the company's aging Rodeo and Trooper. This time around, however, the ads didn't appear so fresh.

Unfortunately for Isuzu, its role in the US market and as part of GM's broader global strategy was never clear. With declining in-house brands, it began to rely more on GM's and Honda's products. But this too would prove shortsighted. In 2002, Honda pulled the plug on its exchange program with Isuzu. The same year, Subaru's parent company bought Isuzu's remaining share of the Lafayette, Indiana assembly facility, leaving Isuzu with no US production base. It was also in 2002 that Isuzu sold its last cars in Canada.

The handwriting was on the wall for Isuzu. With no manufacturing base in the United States and with the appreciation of the yen, previous bestsellers including the Trooper and Rodeo were no longer able to hold onto market share. Its involvement with GM was causing it to slowly bleed to death. In response, Isuzu launched a major stock buyback initiative that concluded with GM's ownership being reduced from 49% to 12%.

Regrettably, the pipeline from Isuzu Japan was ill-suited for the US marketplace. In 2003, facing abysmal US sales, Isuzu discontinued the Rodeo. By 2005, Isuzu dealers had access to only two models: the Ascender, which was based on the GMC Envoy, and the i-series pickup, re-badged from the Chevy Colorado. They also had old Rodeos and Axioms in their inventory. With its dealers averaging only two vehicles sold per month, they were able to stay alive in the United States only through light trucks exported from Japan. In early 2008, Isuzu announced that it would pull out of the US automobile market in January 2009.[5]

SUMMARY COMMENTS

The story of Isuzu is illustrative of the challenges many Japanese companies face as they break into foreign markets. Their success at home leads invariably to interest in and later success at exporting. Their products are first sold as OEM exports, which the overseas importer then brands and distributes, capturing the lion's share of value added. At some point the company tires of this relationship and sets up local manufacturing. Their hope is for faster delivery and greater local responsiveness. But unless they move aggressively, they find that local competitors and dysfunctional partners stymie their efforts. Lacking competent local staff and often short of cash, they outsource either too much or not enough. Progress in winning over customers is slow. At that point, the original entry strategy is open to debate. And with this, roles, performance metrics, and timelines are put on the chopping block. Soon, already weak performance deteriorates further. Hit with mounting losses and a risky future, a retreat is called. Better to be back home amongst friends or at least on familiar ground than be exposed overseas.

While all companies encounter enormous challenges when they move overseas, the challenges are in many ways the most acute for Japanese companies which face unique difficulties brought about by their own culture and history. In the next chapter, we examine the difficulties Japanese companies face, bringing new perspectives and innovation to their regional and global growth challenges. In particular, we focus on the people and leadership challenges of Japanese companies as they attempt to globalize.

6

BARBARIANS AT THE GATE

It is natural and empirically the case that as companies move out of the export stage and put more direct investment into foreign operations that they send expatriate managers from their home country, whether that home country is the United States, Germany, France, Japan, or wherever.[1] However, if firms are going to be successful in the regionalization stage, they need to tap into local and regional knowledge and leadership talent to make the adjustments in product, processes, services, solutions, etc. that fit the needs of the local environment. And as firms move from the regionalization into the globalization stage, they need to tap into the best and brightest talent regardless of passport. This is because no nationality has cornered the market on global leadership talent in general, let alone specific global talent in design, marketing, HR, strategy, or manufacturing. Thus, for companies to move from the export to the regional stage, when it comes to critical human capital, they must overcome their home country national bias. Furthermore, in order to move beyond the regional stage to the borderless global stage, they must become passport blind.

GREATER USE OF HOME COUNTRY EXPATRIATE MANAGERS BY JAPANESE MNCs

A variety of studies have been conducted over the years that have demonstrated that Japanese firms tend to have nearly twice the level of Japanese expatriate managers in their foreign operations than is the case for firms from a number of other countries, including the United States, United Kingdom, Germany, and France.[2]

While few academic studies have looked at this phenomenon longitudinally, data from the Japanese government does provide us with some insights about the deployment of Japanese expatriates over time.

From this, we can look at the deployment of Japanese expatriates from a couple of different angles to get some systematic perspective.

First, we will look at the absolute growth of Japanese expatriates deployed around the world. The Japanese government has tracked the number of Japanese expatriate managers since 1971. No one should be surprised to learn that the total number of Japanese expatriate managers has increased from 84,049 in 1971 to 619,269 in 2003 (the most recent reported year at the time of this book's printing)—a more than six fold increase. While this is interesting, this data doesn't really tell us if the rate of increase of Japanese expatriates is faster, slower, or the same as the increase in international business activities of Japanese firms.

One way to gage this is to look at the overseas revenues per expatriate. Over a period of 30 years, you would expect the revenues-per-expatriate ratio to increase. This is because the longer the foreign affiliate is in place, the larger you would generally expect its revenues to be as it grows. Also, the longer the foreign affiliate is in place, the more mature you would expect its local leaders to become. Consequently, you would also expect the absolute and relative proportion of local leaders to increase over time. Therefore, as the overseas affiliate grows in size, the revenue per home-country expatriate manager should also increase. However, this is not so much what we find with Japanese firms.

Exhibit 6.1 shows the overseas affiliate revenues per Japanese expatriate manager from 1977 through 2002 (the full years in which data

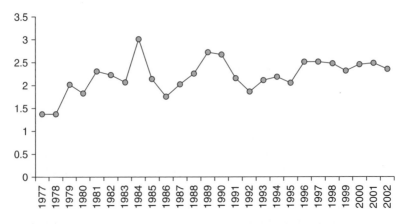

EXHIBIT 6.1 **Overseas Affiliate Revenue per Japanese Expatriate Manager**
Source: Japanese Bureau of Statistics, 2008.

on both overseas affiliate revenues and Japanese expatriate managers are available).

As the chart illustrates, the revenues per Japanese expatriate were lowest in 1977 (¥1.38 billion per expatriate manager) and gradually improved, just as the general logic would suggest and as we see in companies from other countries. The ratio effectively more than doubled to a peak of ¥3 billion in overseas affiliate revenue per expatriate in 1984. Over the next nearly 20 years the ratio bounced around a little but was on average ¥2.28 billion per expatriate, suggesting that the willingness of Japanese firms to bring on and leverage local leaders, let alone to bring in non-Japanese talent as third-country expatriate managers (that is, managers whose nationality is neither Japanese nor that of the local country) has not changed much in two decades.

We also looked at the deployment of Japanese expatriate managers and the utilization of local talent in terms of the number of Japanese expatriate managers per affiliate. Again, over time as the size of foreign affiliates grow and as the numbers of affiliates grow, you would expect the average number of expatriates per affiliate to decline. You would expect this in part because as firms get deeper into regionalization, they would gradually replace home country expatriates with local managers. Further, as you move into globalization, you would expect the number of home country national expatriates per affiliate to decline as third-country expatriates were more widely deployed.

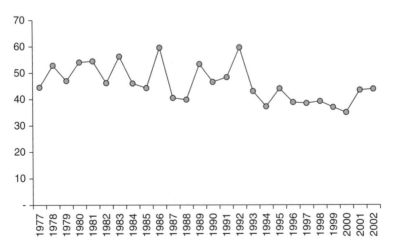

EXHIBIT 6.2 Japanese Expatriates per Japanese Overseas Affiliate
Source: Japan Government Bureau of Statistics, 2008.

As Exhibit 6.2 illustrates, this is not what we find with Japanese companies. The average number of Japanese expatriates per affiliate in 1977 was 45. The average in 2002 (the most recent data at the time of publication) was 44 Japanese expatriates per affiliate. In other words, the number of Japanese expatriates has fluctuated but has not changed in 25 years.

Drivers of low use of local leaders

Why do we find Japanese firms maintaining high levels of home country expatriates over time? A variety of studies have looked at this general phenomenon and point to several factors.[3]

Studies have found that Japanese headquarters exert a much higher level of control over overseas affiliates compared to their US, German, French, British, and other counterparts. Studies have also found that this high level of central control required more frequent communication between the affiliate and HQ. Because of language limitations, the Japanese HQ required these communications be conducted in Japanese. As a consequence, Japanese firms cited the lack of knowledge of Japanese language (written and spoken) by non-Japanese managers as a critical reason for not replacing Japanese expatriates with local managers or third-country expatriates.

Other studies and writings have asserted that Japanese expatriate managers simply don't trust local or third-country managers as they do their own. This lack of trust is cited as the reason for the ongoing high numbers of Japanese expatriate managers.[4] One possible reason cited for a lack of trust is the low level of Japanese language skills on the part of foreigners and weakness of English or other foreign language skills on the part of the Japanese. The lack of trust has also been attributed to simple cross-cultural differences, especially those that in general exist between the "East" (that is, Japan) and the "West" (that is, Europe and the United States).

FOUR PHASES OF EXPATRIATE DEPLOYMENT

In understanding the role of home-country expatriate and local leaders in the transition from the export stage to the regional and global stages, we have identified a four-phase pattern of expatriate deployment. This pattern is not unique to Japanese firms, but the dysfunctions of the pattern seem more common in Japanese firms than others, based on our experience, which includes consulting work with more than 20 Japanese MNCs over the past 25 years, interviews with over 100 Japanese expatriate managers across more than 50 firms, interviews with nearly 150 local and regional non-Japanese managers working for Japanese companies, and interviews with more than 50 top level Japanese global executives.

Phase 1: Send in the experts

Phase 1 occurs in the early stages of overseas expansion in which Japanese firms send Japanese expatriates to set up 'shop' overseas. These expatriates are chosen because they know the Japanese system back home, and their job is to set it up the Japanese way abroad. In manufacturing firms, these individuals typically come from operations and production. Not surprisingly, these managers have worked primarily in Japan, with Japanese employees, and only speak Japanese. Their entire career has been with one company. They are completely loyal to the parent company. And to ensure their allegiances remain dutifully directed to the parent company and to make sure they don't get too lonely, often teams of like-minded Japanese are sent in.

It is easy to understand why this approach makes sense to the Japanese. After all, the Japanese way has worked at home and made the economy the second largest in the world. Furthermore, the Japanese way has worked abroad, in that products made at home have been successfully exported overseas.

Of course some local employees must be hired. But, who should be hired? What type of local leaders should be selected? If your job is to come in and to explain the system to people and tell them what to do and how to do it the Mitsubishi, Canon, or Daiei way, then you naturally will look for and hire people who take direction, who listen, and who obey. As a consequence, the early Japanese expatriates tend to look for local managers who are willing to say "yes," and do what they are told. However, the fruits of future frustration are sewn in these seeds of initial success.

Phase 2: Look for high caliber locals

Phase 2 comes when the Japanese expatriates begin to recognize that to maximize their local sales they need to make some modifications to their products, services, processes, and even management systems. They look to their local managers whom they hired in Phase 1 but find them lacking. They view them as just "doers", not thinkers or leaders. So, often they go out and hire some higher level and higher caliber local managers. In this phase, Japanese firms are looking for leaders who know the local market and have proven track records at achieving results, especially in terms of marketing and sales. These high-caliber leaders exist and can be found in virtually any major country in which Japanese MNCs operate. Our experience and the data from our interviews clearly suggest that when Japanese firms go looking for these local leaders, they indeed find them and with the right financial package can hire them.

Phase 3: Local success and frustration

Phase 3 is centered on these higher caliber local managers making the needed modifications, adjustments, etc. to the original line of products and services and sometimes even coming up with new ones that better fit the market. However, these local non-Japanese managers discover that almost regardless of their business results, they will not be considered for most significant regional roles and certainly will not have a future at the global, corporate level (see The Story of James below). After all, they are not Japanese; they do not speak or read Japanese; they do not think like Japanese; they do not act like Japanese.

THE STORY OF JAMES

During a recent research visit to the United Kingdom, we met with a man we'll call James, the CEO of a subsidiary of large Japanese industrial products company. James's business unit employed 1,800 people and he had responsibility for a manufacturing facility which was located several hundred kilometers from London.

During our discussion, we mentioned to James that we would be traveling to Japan and meeting with his Japanese boss just two weeks later. His face turned bright red. James then asked the following question: "Could you please ask him how he thinks I am doing?" Our reply: "Why don't you ask him yourself?" And then he said the following: "I always ask him this question. And he always tells me the same thing—that I am doing fine. But I don't believe him. It

---

isn't that I am doing badly, but that he just doesn't open up to me. He doesn't tell me anything." We then asked how much autonomy he had in the United Kingdom. His response: "Not much. I make what they tell me to make. I have no ability to customize anything for either the UK or the EU."

Then, our next question: "How long have you worked for the company?" His reply: "I have been with them my entire career. In fact, I am the most senior non-Japanese in the company. Just last year they started to invite me to Japan four times per year for meetings. But these aren't very helpful because they are all in Japanese and so I sit in the back with the interpreter."

And then we asked: "Where do you go from here, career-wise? What are your prospects for the future?" His reply: "Nowhere. My career has reached its zenith. I don't speak Japanese. Heaven knows I have tried to learn, but it just doesn't stick. But even if I did speak Japanese, it wouldn't matter. They won't let me into their circle because I am not one of them. And I never will be. To be honest, I only got this far because I am a humble servant. If I were to start agitating for more local autonomy, it just wouldn't be tolerated. This is the end of the line for me."

Phase 4: Best and brightest leave

In Phase 4 many of the best and brightest who have global leadership ambitions and believe they have global capabilities recognize their limitations in the Japanese MNCs and look for opportunities to leave. Interestingly, when you talk to the departing foreign executives and to the senior Japanese executives back in the home office, you would swear that they must come from different universes or at least that one sees the world through infrared while the other sees it through ultraviolet lenses because their view of the same situation is that different. Recently, a departing senior US executive who spoke quite reasonable Japanese said to us when asked why he was leaving his Japanese company:

The senior executives in Osaka just don't get it. They think that if you cannot mold your thinking and career aspirations to theirs that you are disloyal and selfish. I'm moving on because I will never be accepted as an equal. The job that I am leaving for is in my view a natural progression but it is one that if I stayed in this company, I would never be given. No one but a Japanese has ever held that position and no one but a Japanese ever will. Maybe I'm not good enough for it, but I've lived in Japan for over three years and speak the language; I love the country and the culture. If someone like me cannot be considered for that global role, I'm not sure who could.

When we spoke to a key executive in the home office about this person's departure, we got a very different world view:

"Bob"[not his real name] doesn't get it. We had high hopes for him to soon return to his home country (the US) and take up a significant position there. Having spent time in Japan, he could have performed a vital function and been an important link between HQ and the affiliate. We're disappointed given all our investment in him. Given his interest in Japan, I was surprised that he so easily focused on money and a promotion and would leave us. We will be careful before we repeat this mistake again.

As the last sentence hints at, at that point, there is often a reintroduction of Japanese expatriate managers because clearly the locals cannot be trusted to be loyal over their entire career. It thus becomes a self-perpetuating model. Only the Japanese can run Japanese affiliates, let alone take on any global responsibilities.

In pointing out this pattern, we want to emphasize that holding onto foreign top executives is a challenge for every company. We have seen this pattern in MNCs from the United States, Germany, France, the United Kingdom, Finland, Korea, Spain, and many other countries. However, our experience indicates that the problem is by far the most acute in Japanese firms.

THE BAMBOO CEILING

In pointing out this pattern, we want to make two things perfectly clear. First, we know of no scientific and comprehensive research that shows that Japanese firms lose non-home national executives at a higher rate that is the case in US, German, French, or other firms. However, an absence of research doesn't mean that there isn't a problem. Second, as we said we have seen this pattern in MNCs besides Japanese firms; they are not alone. Nevertheless, the anecdotal evidence abounds that the problem is most acute in Japanese firms.

Our MBA students see it all the time. In our interactions over the years with literally thousands of MBA graduates, there is a clear perception (rightly or wrongly) that if you have global leadership ambitions and are not Japanese, do not plan to work for a Japanese firm other than as an early or mid-career springboard. In encountering this perception nearly 20 years ago, the lead author of this book coined the term "bamboo ceiling." Bamboo ceiling essentially captures the notion that if you are not Japanese you can go only so far and no further in a Japanese company.

We could put some of this debate to rest if there were systematic and comprehensive empirical evidence to show that Japanese firms have a lower representation of non-home country nationals at their global senior executive level than US, German, French, or other firms and that having greater national and cultural diversity among the top executives enhances a firm's internationalization and performance. Sadly, the definitive empirical evidence is not there to totally put this debate to bed, but there are some alarming findings.

First, there is growing empirical evidence that greater national diversity of top management teams is associated with both greater levels of internationalization and with higher global performance.[5] Second, there is directional evidence that Japanese MNCs have a lower percentage of foreign top executives than other MNCs. For example, a recent study examined over 350 European companies with more than 1,000 employees and over 500 million in annual revenue. The study consisted of over 7,000 individual top executive observations from 2000 to 2005.[6] The study found a significant and growing percentage of non-home country nationals (that is, foreigners) among the top executives. Specifically, they found that the average of foreigners among the top executives for Swiss firms was 39%, for Dutch firms 27%, for Swedish firms 18%, for UK firms 16%, and for Finnish firms 10%.

We know of no systematic study of nationality of Japanese top executive teams, so we conducted our own small study. We looked at the top 10 Japanese firms listed in the *Fortune Global 500* for 2008 and examined the nationality of all the top executives listed in the Annual Reports for those companies. We selected these firms because arguably they should be some of the most global. Those companies in rank order were Toyota Motor, Honda Motor, Hitachi, Nissan Motor, Nippon Telegraph & Telephone, Matsushita Electric Industrial, Sony, Toshiba, Nippon Life Insurance, and Nippon Oil. On average each company listed 25 top executives. On average only 5.5% of these executives were non-Japanese. However, if you exclude Nissan and Sony from the analysis (both of which had foreign executives introduced because of severe crises within the companies), then 100% of the senior executives were Japanese and 0% were foreigners.

CONCLUSION

In summary, while the domestic and export stages provide the benefit of working with people you know, trust, and with whom you share a common culture, heritage, education system, and language, these can also act as inhibitors to progressing into the regionalization stage and onward into the global stage of development. If you are going to grow through geographic expansion in the regional stage, you need to tap into local and regional talent outside your home country. You require these people to help you understand the customers, competitors, employees, regulators, partners, and general communities in these foreign markets. If you are going to grow through market share expansion in the global stage, you need to tap into the best and brightest talent anywhere and everywhere in the world you can find it—not just in your home country. Otherwise, you will not capture the diversity of perspective, experience, and expertise necessary for innovative breakthroughs. As we said, no country or culture has cornered the market on marketing, strategy, logistics, supply chain management, finance, or any other area of expertise. As a consequence, if you are going to be innovative and grow through market expansion, you have no choice but to tap into the best human capital wherever you can find it—you have to become passport blind.

Sadly, Japanese MNCs are failing to fully access foreign talent at the local, regional, and certainly global levels. As we noted, with very rare exception, the senior global executives in Japanese MNCs are all Japanese, which is increasingly *not* the case for North American and European MNCs.

7

WATER, WATER EVERYWHERE, BUT NOT A DROP TO DRINK

Having a large and homogeneous population seems to have facilitated Japan's rise throughout the 1960s, 1970s, 1980s, and into the 1990s. It created a cohesive workforce that increased both the production and quality of products that enabled success at home and exports abroad. However, as Japanese firms tried to move from a domestic plus export oriented business platform toward regional and global platforms, the homogeneous workforce of Japan and lack of experience with foreigners relative to other major economic powers such as the United States, Germany, France, and the United Kingdom turned a former advantage into a disadvantage.

As we discussed earlier, dealing effectively with people from different countries, cultures, ethnicities, languages, etc., is key to moving effectively into and succeeding in the regionalization and globalization stages of growth. You need to relate to the different people around the world in order to expand into their countries. And you have little choice but to tap into and bring together people of diverse background in order to spark the innovation needed to create and expand market share where you are already present.

The sad facts are that if you grow up in Japan you simply don't have the opportunity to gain significant experience with diversity compared to the opportunities in many other countries. For example, Exhibit 7.1 shows the proportion of foreigners residing in Japan, Germany, France, United Kingdom, and United States.

If you do some simple calculations, you see that the United Kingdom and France with less than half the population of Japan have more than twice as many foreigners living within their borders. While the percentage of foreigners has been increasing in Japan, it still lags far behind other countries. The point of this book is not to determine whether the reason for the low number of foreigners is due to Japanese

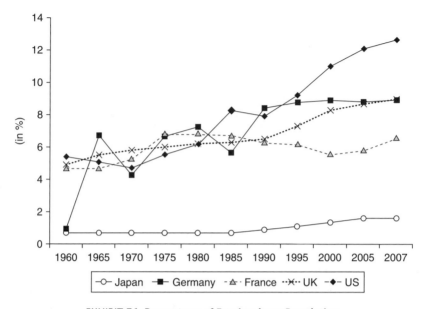

EXHIBIT 7.1 **Percentage of Foreign-born Population**
Sources: Japanese Bureau of Statistics 2008; France Insee recensements de la population, 2007;
United Kingdom National Statistics, 2008; US Census Bureau, 2008.

and Japan being unwelcoming of non-Japanese or if non-Japanese are biased against Japan, or anything else. We will leave that diagnosis to others. From a pragmatic business standpoint, it does not really matter why it has been that way in the past and is this way today. What matters most is that if dealing effectively with foreigners requires some experience, then growing up in Japan puts you at a natural disadvantage because the opportunities are just not as plentiful as in other countries.

One might wonder if living in a great metropolitan city like Tokyo would make a difference. Sadly, the answer is no. About 2% of Tokyo's 13 million residents are foreigners. While this is somewhat higher than in Japan in general, it is low compared to other cities, such as the greater New York City in which 8 million residents (36% of the total) are foreign-born. This means that there are 10 times as many foreigners living in New York as in metropolitan Tokyo. A similar contrast can be found in Singapore. There are approximately 4.5 million residents in the city-state of Singapore. In 2007, 30% of them were foreigners. That means a total of 1.35 million foreigners live in Singapore, which is more than all the foreigners living in Japan—a country with 28 times the total population of Singapore.

While this general picture is not so bright, what if we dig deeper into the details? For example, research suggests early experiences with diversity, especially interacting with foreigners, has a bigger impact on an individual than experiences later in life.[1] As a consequence, we might wonder about the number of Japanese children living with their parents outside of Japan and therefore getting these formidable experiences. Maybe this is the key.

To assist in investigating this possibility, we turned to the Ministry of Education in Japan which reports a number of relevant statistics. First, Exhibit 7.2 presents the number of Japanese elementary, middle, and high school students that have returned from abroad.

As the chart shows, the absolute number of Japanese students returning to elementary and middle schools rose between 1990 and 1995 and then declined through 2005 with a very small uptick in 2007. The number of students returning to high schools has remained relatively stable from 1990 through 2007.

While the previous exhibit shows the absolute numbers of children returning from abroad, Exhibit 7.3 shows what percentage of those returning students represent relative to the total enrollment of Japanese elementary, middle, and high school students in Japan. This chart shows that Japanese students returning from abroad represented a miniscule percentage of the total number of students in Japanese schools. The peak for elementary students was in 2000, and the returning elementary students represented about 1/10th of 1% of the total elementary students in Japan. That means that only 1 in 1000 elementary students

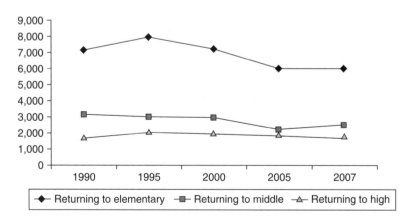

EXHIBIT 7.2 **Number of Japanese Elementary, Middle, and High School Students Returning to Japan**
Source: Japan Bureau of Statistics, 2008.

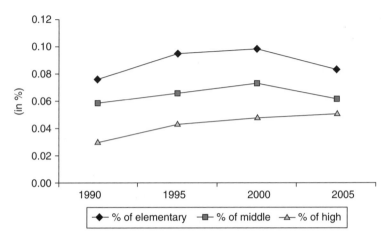

EXHIBIT 7.3 **Japanese Students Returning to Japan as a Percentage of Total Japanese Students Enrolled in Japan**
Source: Japan Bureau of Statistics, 2008.

had returned from abroad. The peak for middle school students was also in 2000, and the returning middle school students represented about 7/10th of 1% of the total middle school students in Japan. The peak for high school students occurred in 2005 when the returning high school students represented about 5/10th of 1% of the total high school students in Japan.

We can better gage the aggregate potential foreign experience of these Japanese elementary, middle, and high school students by looking at the total number that are abroad, not just the number returning. Sadly, the Japanese government only provides records for total number of Japanese elementary and middle school students abroad. No data is available for high school students. Exhibit 7.4 shows both the total number of Japanese elementary and middle school students abroad and the percentage they represent of the total Japanese elementary and middle school students enrolled in Japan. As Exhibit 7.4 shows, the total number of elementary and middle school students has gone up by 12.6%. However, they still only represent about 1/2 of 1% of the total of Japanese schoolchildren.

When we dig even further, we find that many of these Japanese elementary and middle school students abroad are not getting the expected and full opportunity to interact with foreigners. Exhibit 7.5 shows the percentage of Japanese elementary and middle school students abroad who are enrolled not in the public schools of the country in which they reside or even in the international schools within the

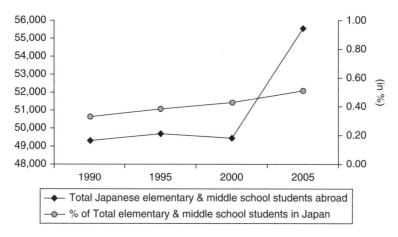

EXHIBIT 7.4 Japanese Elementary and Middle School Students Abroad
Source: Japan Bureau of Statistics, 2008.

EXHIBIT 7.5 Japanese Elementary and Middle
School Students Enrolled Full-Time in Japanese
Schools Abroad

Year	Percentage enrolled full-time in Japanese schools while abroad
1990	37.1
1995	37.3
2000	33.8
2005	31.8
2007	32.0

Source: Japan Bureau of Statistics, 2008.

foreign country of residence but are enrolled full-time in dedicated Japanese schools.

As Exhibit 7.5 shows, on average about 1 in 3 Japanese elementary and middle school students are enrolled full-time in a Japanese school while they are overseas. The reasons for this are many and legitimate. For example, in our research and other studies of Japanese families, many parents cited the lock-step education system in Japan and the disadvantages children experience if they get out of step while they are with their parents residing in a foreign country as a key reason why they enrolled their children in a full-time Japanese school while away.[2] However, our point is not that Japanese parents may have valid reasons for enrolling their children in full-time Japanese schools while overseas but that the true opportunity for Japanese elementary and middle school students

71

to gain experience with foreigners is limited by this. As a consequence, it is not 5/10th of 1% of Japanese elementary and middle schoolchildren that are getting a chance to interact intensively with foreigners while abroad but only about 3/10th of 1%.

WHAT ABOUT OLDER STUDENTS?

While early childhood experiences tend to be formative, the research also suggests that experiences interacting with foreigners later in life can also have an impact. To better understand this, we looked at the rate of foreign college students studying in Japan and of Japanese college students studying abroad. On these dimensions, unlike with elementary aged children, some international comparisons can more readily be made. Exhibit 7.6 shows the number of foreign students

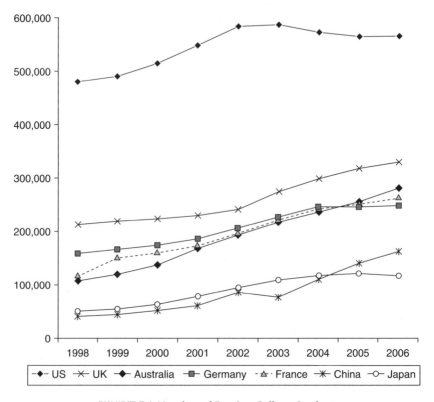

EXHIBIT 7.6 **Number of Foreign College Students**
Source: OECD Student Mobility.

enrolled in college in each of seven countries with the largest number of foreign students.

As Exhibit 7.6 illustrates, the number of foreign college students is generally increasing across all the major markets, except Japan where the numbers have flattened out and slightly declined. It is interesting to note that nearly 50% of the total foreign student population in Japan comes from just one country—China.

Perhaps more telling than just the total number of foreign students is the percentage of the total that these foreign students represent. In general, the higher the percentage, the more likely the chance home country nationals will interact and gain experience with foreigners. Exhibit 7.7 provides this information for the most recently available figures for the key countries except China (for which comparable data is difficult to verify).

As the chart clearly indicates, if you want to encounter foreigners and gain that experience as a college student, the best place to do this is Singapore and the worst place is Japan. Clearly having English as the language of college instruction is a benefit in drawing foreign students as illustrated by the United Kingdom, Australia, and Singapore, which have the largest percentage of foreign students. The exception to this pattern is the United States, which is working from a much larger base of college students.

Having foreign college students come to your country is one way of gaining experience but going out and studying abroad is another, even more powerful way. Exhibit 7.8 provides some comparisons of the number of Japanese college students studying abroad compared to

EXHIBIT 7.7 **Foreign College Students as a Percentage of Total**

Country	Percentage
Japan	2.9
US	3.9
Germany	12.4
France	11.0
UK	15.8
Australia	21.1
Singapore	38.2

Sources: Japan Bureau of Statistics, 2008; Singapore Ministry of Education, 2008; OECD Student Mobility.

EXHIBIT 7.8 **Students Studying Abroad**

Country	Students studying abroad	Study abroad/ Total students (in %)
US	217,920	1.5
Germany	62,000	3.1
Japan	60,474	1.5
France	49,749	2.3
UK	23,134	1.0

Sources: Japan Bureau of Statistics, 2008; OECD Student Mobility.

four other major countries and the percentage of the country's total college student population who are studying abroad.

As the table indicates, in terms of raw numbers, the United States has the largest group of students studying in foreign countries by a wide margin. However, as a percentage of the total, the United States and Japan have about the same percentage of their college students studying in other countries.

CONCLUSIONS

In this chapter and the previous two chapters, we have presented a fair amount of data. So what can we conclude from all the numbers? Several factors seem to have inhibited Japanese MNCs from moving more fully into the regionalization and globalization stages. These include:

- Generally poor financial performance from their affiliates abroad.
- Generally lower tolerance for risk that may have further hurt their motivation to invest abroad.
- A preference for home-national, Japanese expatriates, and the inability to recruit or retain the best and the brightest local managers.
- A preference for home-national, Japanese global executives, and a lack of high caliber foreign executives at the top.
- Low levels of experience working with foreigners in Japan because of the low numbers of foreigners in Japan as workers or as students.
- Low levels of experience with foreigners because of the small numbers of Japanese children or college students spending time abroad and low levels of Japanese children interacting with foreigners while abroad due to their enrollment in overseas Japanese schools.

Given all of this, it is not surprising that Japanese MNCs simply have not grown at the rate of MNCs based in the United States, United Kingdom, Germany, France, etc. We predict that this relatively lower rate of overall growth will continue unless Japanese executives focus a majority of their attention outside of Japan. This will require overcoming many of the barriers we have identified in the last three chapters.

But so far, we have focused heavily on numbers and data. What does all this look like at the ground level from an individual's perspective? In the next chapter, we provide a more personal view of what has happened (and not happened) in Japanese MNCs in contrast to their North American and European counterparts by looking at the careers of two people who grew up and joined companies in two different cities that were world's apart.

8

A TALE OF TWO CITIES

So far we have reviewed the incredible success of the Japanese in the 1980s and early 1990s and examined the factors that have inhibited their movement into the regional and global stages of development. In this chapter, we review these forces from the real-life stories of two leaders at two very different companies. While the company names remain unaltered, we have disguised the names of the individuals to protect confidentialities.

THE STORIES OF KENICHI TANAKA AND JEAN-LOUIS DESVIGNES

In 1988, in two different cities half a world away, two aspiring and ambitious young men graduated from university and started their careers. The first, Kenichi Tanaka, grew up in Osaka, Japan and joined Daiei; the other, Jean-Louis Desvignes, grew up in Paris and joined Carrefour.

Kenichi Tanaka was a dedicated fan of the Daiei Hawks, one of the major league baseball teams in Japan. After working very hard in high school and scoring well on his college entrance exam test, Tanaka was the pride of his family when he was accepted to Kyoto University, not far from his home. As Tanaka approached graduation, he felt his upbeat personality would fit best with a growing and dynamic company. He decided that joining the largest retailer in Japan would be a smart move. His family was proud of his choice and was happy to tell friends and family about his good fortune. Given the breadth and size of Daiei, it looked as though Tanaka would have secure and exciting career opportunities.

Jean-Louis Desvignes grew up in the Paris suburb of Antony. Given his family background (his father was French but his mother was Greek) and the fact that they were middle class but certainly not wealthy, his family was absolutely thrilled and surprised when he was accepted into one of the most prestigious universities in all of France—the *Ecole Nationale d'Administration*. Desvignes worked harder than most of his classmates in school and did well in his classes. As graduation approached, he felt that he wanted a career that would be dynamic and potentially stretch him beyond the borders of his homeland that he loved. By chance, an older brother of a classmate introduced him to an opportunity at Carrefour. When Desvignes told his family of his choice, they were not so thrilled and had hoped that he would have joined one of the government ministries or a blue chip company such as Michelin or Rhone Poulenc. Carrefour was seen by Desvignes's parents as a down-market, no-frills discount retailer and one that recently had to withdraw from the United Kingdom and Belgium because it just couldn't compete effectively in those markets.

Tanaka at Daiei

Tanaka joined Daiei in 1988 nearly 30 years after it was founded by Isao Nakauchi, the son of a pharmacist, as a pharmacy store not long after the end of the Korean War in 1957.[1] The year 1957 was not an easy time to start a business in Japan because US purchases from Japanese manufacturers dropped significantly after the Korean War. In fact, about this time the general Japanese economy went into a major downturn. However, Nakauchi discovered that if he bought surpluses from overextended manufacturers at rock-bottom prices and passed the savings on to consumers, the cash-strapped consumers rewarded his store by coming in droves. As a consequence, Nakauchi quickly expanded the wares of the store beyond those of a traditional pharmacy. This merchandise expansion proved very successful, and throughout the 1960s Nakauchi continued to expand the diversity of products carried in his stores and subsequently increased the number of Daiei stores across the country.

In 1972, Daiei celebrated its 15th anniversary and operated 75 superstores. In just 15 years, it had grown from one store to become Japan's largest supermarket operator and second largest retailer. An important and additional piece of its growth story in the 1970s came from Nakauchi recognizing that many goods made in Japan were selling abroad for less than they were at home. As a consequence, Nakauchi struck several deals in which he bought Japanese-made consumer goods and relabeled them under the Daiei brand and sold them for significantly less (sometimes 50% less) than they sold for in Japan under the Japanese "name brand." For example, he struck a deal with Crown Radio of Japan in which he bought Crown TV sets, rebranded them as Daiei TVs and sold them for half of what Crown brand TVs were selling for in Japan.

In addition to breakneck growth at home, Daiei also ventured abroad in the early 1970s. In 1972, Daiei created Daiei USA as a wholly owned subsidiary and opened a store in Honolulu, Hawaii. The company later bought Holiday Mart, a three-store discount chain in Honolulu.

At home, Daiei also worked to diversify its base. It entered into two key joint ventures and opened branches of US department store Joseph Magnin and also Swift & Company's Dipper Dan Ice Cream Shoppe in Japan. With this growth, in 1974, Daiei surpassed Mitsukoshi to become the largest retailer in Japan. That same year in an effort to grow its Daiei store sales, Daiei began selling US retailer J.C. Penney's merchandise in its own stores in Japan. In 1976, Daiei and J.C. Penney entered into a joint venture to open stores in Japan under the American company's name. In 1978, in an effort to continually expand the base of sales within its stores, Daiei added merchandise from UK retailer Marks and Spencer to its own store offerings.

Beginning in 1979 and then throughout the 1980s, Daiei expanded from retailing into restaurants. For example, it joined with Wendy's International to open Wendy's fast-food restaurants in Japan. By 1988, Daiei was running 30 restaurants throughout Japan.

Like many Japanese companies, Nakauchi financed this expansion primarily through debt, with the expectation that future growth would provide the cash to service the debt. However, in 1984 and 1985 the company lost money primarily due to its high borrowing costs. The company reorganized and returned to profitability in 1986 and was strong enough in 1987 to acquire Riccar, a sewing machine manufacturer.

When Tanaka joined Daiei in 1988, the company was not only the largest retailer in Japan but it also controlled nearly 20% of all the grocery market in the country. It was seen as a pioneer of the "every day low prices" concept in Japan and was loved by consumers for its great bargains. After a two-year rotation across several areas of the company, Tanaka was placed into a small unit that was formulating plans to open Japan's first wholesale membership club, similar to Wal-Mart's Sam's Club. Although Tanaka's role was small, he was proud to have been part of the team that launched the first club wholesale store in Japan in 1992.

After working on this project for four years, Tanaka moved to the international division, a move some members of his family saw as risky since sales outside Japan did not even account for 10% of the total. While working in the International Department located in Osaka, Tanaka participated in the acquisition of a supermarket in Hawaii in 1994, the expansion of the Ala Moana Center shopping mall in Honolulu about the same time, and the establishment of Daiei's first joint venture in China in 1995.

While these international activities were a small part of the total, Tanaka was very proud to be working for Daiei. In 1995, Daiei had sales of over ¥3 trillion and was #73 on the *Fortune Global 500* list, and was among the 30 largest companies of any type in all of Japan.[2] Tanaka was riding high and felt that Daiei was destined to dominate not only Japan but also hoped that with continued international expansion would some day dominate much of the world.

International expansion

In late 1995, when Tanaka approached his bosses about international expansion outside of Hawaii, he was met with resistance. Tanaka cited Jardine Matheson (a conglomerate based in Hong Kong) and the growth of its Dairy Farm division across Asia. Dairy Farm's Cold Storage grocery unit was emerging as the dominant grocer in Singapore. Its Giant unit was expanding rapidly in Malaysia. In addition, he noted that Carrefour was pushing into China, Taiwan, and Malaysia and Wal-Mart was pushing into China and Korea. Tanaka reminded his superiors that these competitors were pushing into Asia because the economies in the region were booming. His supervisors reminded him that none of these foreigners were having any success in Japan and that the Japanese economy at the time was nearly *twice* as large as the economies of Australia, New Zealand, India, Indonesia, Singapore, Malaysia, Thailand, Vietnam, Philippines, Hong Kong, Taiwan, South Korea, and China combined! Or seen from a Western European perspective, the Japanese economy in 1995 was larger than that of Germany, France, and the United Kingdom *combined*.

When Tanaka asked about the need to tap into the human capital and talent in these Asian countries, he was met with near contempt by his superiors. He was told that even Daiei's best managers in the United States were only capable of taking orders from the head office in Osaka. Foreigners simply could not understand a Japanese company well enough to take up significant leadership roles. The message to Tanaka was that while Daiei might continue its modest investments internationally, those opportunities compared to the ones at home just did not stack up. After all, in 1995, Japan was the second largest economy in the world with a GDP of $5.3 trillion at current prices and accounted for about 15% of global GDP. Why should the company look abroad when there was so much opportunity at home?

Stagnation

The stagnation that started when the real estate and stock market bubble burst in 1991 was given a further push with the Asian currency crisis in 1997. The combination and cumulative effect finally caught up to Daiei and hit the company hard. Nominal GDP in Japan dropped dramatically: in 1995 it was $5.24 trillion; in 1996 it had dropped to $4.62 trillion; in 1997 it had fallen again to $4.23 trillion; by 1998 it had sunk to $3.84 trillion. Daiei's concentration of assets and other activities in Japan caused it to feel the full force of the country's downturn. In order to meet its debt obligations, Daiei had to raise cash by selling much of its holdings in the United States, including the Alo Moana Center shopping mall in Hawaii. Tanaka saw his role shift almost overnight from growing the international division to selling off most of Daiei's overseas assets.

As Daiei continued to restructure and sell off assets, in 2000 it lost its leading retailer title to 7-Eleven Japan Co.[3] An insider trading scandal that year caused further trouble. Tadasu Toba resigned as president of the company (but remained as a director of the firm); founder Nakauchi also resigned (but remained an advisor to the firm).[4] Kunio Takagi, a Daiei executive, was appointed the new president. Takagi announced (1) the issuance of ¥120 billion in new shares to raise cash, (2) the closure of 32 outlets, and (3) the elimination of 4,000 job over a three-year period to reduce costs. He also announced the sale of most of Daiei's holdings in Lawson, its large, national convenience store franchise.[5]

Because of its nearly total reliance on the home market, the general stagnation of the Japanese economy from 1991 through 2005 and the overall decline in consumer spending took its toll on Daiei. The company's problems were no-doubt compounded by the high costs of its debt burden built at a time when domestic growth seemed unstoppable. As a consequence, in 10 short years, Daiei went from its peak in 1995 on the *Fortune Global 500* list at #73 to #353 by 2005.

More challenges for Tanaka

By 2005, Tanaka had already moved out of the International Division and into the Personnel Division, where his international downsizing experience was utilized in supervising domestic store closures and layoffs. In May 2005, Daiei Inc. shareholders at their annual general meeting approved a new management team to help rebuild the struggling retailer under guidance of the government-backed Industrial Revitalization Corp. of Japan. Takagi was replaced by Yasuyuki Higuchi, 47, the former president of Hewlett-Packard Japan Ltd., as Daiei president and chief operating officer. Fumiko Hayashi, 59, former president of BMW Tokyo Corp., was appointed as chairwoman and chief executive officer.[6] Later that year the founder of Daiei, Isao Nakauchi, died at the age of 83 from a stroke.

In the shadow of the loss of the founder, the new team laid out a further restructuring plan. But despite the new team's efforts, the negative momentum was too much to overcome. The next year in 2006, Daiei dropped further on the *Fortune Global 500* list from #353 to #452. Later that same year, Marubeni, which was Daiei's largest shareholder, initiated the removal of Yasuyuki Higuchi as president less than two years into his tenure and installed Toru Nishimi as president.[7] Fumiko Hayashi stayed on, but was released as CEO because the post was abolished. Instead, she was named as an advisor to the firm. In 2006, Daiei closed one of its largest stores in a district next to Makuhari on the outskirts of Tokyo because the much larger US discount retailer Costco and French hypermarket specialist Carrefour were stealing away too many customers.

A year later in 2007, Aeon became Daiei's largest shareholder and decided that even further leadership changes were required.[8] Aeon board member, Yoshiharu Kawato, became chairman of Daiei Inc. and replaced Fumiko Hayashi, who became vice chairwoman of Daiei. Kawato was a retail industry veteran with more than 40 years of experience who had led the growth of Aeon, the top-ranked operator of general merchandise stores in Japan. Aeon Senior Vice President Akinori Yamashita also joined the new Daiei management team as a managing director. Despite these additional leadership changes, in 2007 Daiei fell off the *Fortune Global 500* list. Perhaps seeing the writing on the wall, in 2008, Hayashi left Daiei and joined Nissan as a Corporate Vice President.

By mid-2009, Tanaka, 43, was thinking the unthinkable in Japan— should he leave Daiei to join another company? Whereas when he joined the company in 1988, he smiled with pride when people asked where he worked, now instead of pride, Tanaka felt shame in stating he worked for Daiei. His beloved Daiei Hawk professional baseball team had been sold to the internet service provider Softbank.[9] He had seen the company's stock price fall from nearly ¥3,000 in late 2005 to just over ¥300 by mid-2009. Unlike the case of Nissan, which nearly 10 years earlier had brought in a foreigner, Carlos Ghosn, at the insistence of Renault, Nissan's largest shareholder, and successfully turned things around, all the leadership changes at the top of Daiei had not turned the company around and the firm was still struggling to stay alive. In fact, from what Tanaka knew, it looked as though sales would drop and losses would mount yet again in 2009. Like the blossoms on a *Sakura* tree after full bloom, it seemed to Tanaka that the prospects for Daiei, and perhaps his career, were destined fall and then get carried off and forgotten with the winds of change.

Desvignes at Carrefour

The company that Desvignes joined in 1988 got its start just two years after Daiei.[10] Carrefour (French for "intersection") was created by the Fournier and Defforey families in 1959. Carrefour opened its first supermarket in Annecy, Haute-Savoie (near the French alps) the next year in 1960. The following year, LLC Promodis, the forerunner of Promodes, which was created through the merger of two whole-saler families from Normandy, managed by Paul-Auguste Halley and Leonor Duval-Lemonnier, was brought into the Carrefour group. The following year (1962) Promodes opened its first supermarket in Mantes-la-Ville (Yvelines). In 1963, Carrefour invented a new store concept: the hypermarket. The first Carrefour hypermarket opened in Sainte-Genevieve-des-bois, offering food and non-food items with a floor area of 2,500 square meters, which was more than twice the size of the average supermarket at the time.

As the 1960s came to a close, Carrefour saw increased competition and some potential legal restrictions on large retail outlets at home and potential growth opportunities in neighboring markets. In 1969, Carrefour's Promodes supermarket adopted the more neutral-sounding Champion brand name for international expansion and the company also pushed the Carrefour hypermarket concept outside France to Belgium.

The 1970s saw a number of important developments. First, in 1970 Carrefour shares were listed on the Paris stock exchange. The next year, the Promodes hypermarkets adopted the Continent banner name. Carrefour also consolidated its convenience stores under the Shopi banner. In 1973, Carrefour opened its first hypermarket in Spain and in 1975 Carrefour opened its first hypermarket in Brazil. In 1976,

Carrefour introduced *"produits libres,"* which were unbranded products with the value proposition that they were "just as good, but cheaper" than branded products.

The 1980s saw Carrefour continue its growth at home while accelerating its growth abroad. In 1981, it opened its first Continent hypermarket in Porto, Portugal. The next year Carrefour opened its first hypermarket in Argentina. With its growth and size, Carrefour saw the opportunity to buy directly from manufacturers and then rebrand products under the Carrefour name, which it began in 1985. In 1988 Carrefour acquired the 128 supermarkets of the Primisteres group to add to its Champion supermarket division. And the next year, Carrefour opened its first hypermarket in Taiwan.

When Desvignes joined Carrefour in 1988, unlike Daiei in Japan, Carrefour was not the largest retailer in France, but it was emerging as one of the more international and that is what appealed to Desvignes. And so after going through the 24-month management training program that gave him exposure to different aspects of the company, Desvignes lobbied to be assigned to the international division. No sooner did he land there in 1990 than he discovered that the company was making preparations for the launch of their first hypermarket in Greece. Desvignes was delighted with this news because while his father was French, his mother was Greek, and Desvignes spoke some Greek.

International expansion

Throughout the 1990s, Desvignes saw his world change dramatically as Carrefour pushed international expansion. By 1995, Carrefour had 968 stores across its hypermarket, supermarket, and convenience categories in 11 different countries across Europe, South America, and Asia. In terms of overall sales revenues, it was #95 on the *Fortune Global 500* list.

Carrefour accelerated its push into Asia throughout the remainder of the 1990s. In addition to the stores it had already set up in China, Taiwan, and Malaysia, between 1995 and 2000 the company added stores in Thailand, Korea, Hong Kong, Singapore, and Indonesia. By early 2000, Carrefour had 23 stores in Taiwan, 20 in China, 12 in Korea, 9 in Thailand, 6 in Malaysia, 5 in Indonesia, 4 in Hong Kong, and 1 in Singapore.

International assignment

After 10 years, working on international marketing and logistics issues primarily for the Carrefour hypermarket stores throughout Europe, in

83

1998, Desvignes was approached about taking an international assignment. He was offered opportunities in both Latin America and Asia. If he chose Latin America, he would likely be assigned to Argentina or Mexico. Since he spoke Spanish due to his work helping the significant expansion in Spain and since his wife also spoke some Spanish from her studies at university, there was some appeal to jobs in Argentina or Mexico. For Asia, he had the option of Singapore or Japan. Singapore represented the easiest family option. More than 70% of the French multinationals had their regional headquarters in Singapore and as a consequence, there were excellent French schools, restaurants, and a strong French expatriate community. However, the job of helping the one store there become more successful was not so interesting to Desvignes. Japan, on the other hand, was more exciting. Although it represented a difficult challenge for the family because none of them spoke Japanese, the opportunity of launching Carrefour in Japan, the second largest economy in the world, was for Desvignes just too good to pass up. Within just a few months of accepting the Japan job, Desvignes, his wife Maria, and their young son set off for Tokyo.

Desvignes's soaring flight to Japan in 1998 was almost a perfect metaphor for the rise of Carrefour globally. In five short years from 1995 to 2000, Carrefour had risen from #95 to #37 on the *Fortune Global 500* list. During the same period, Daiei had fallen from #73 to #162 on the *Fortune* list. Desvignes worked hard on the launch of the first Carrefour store which took place in December of 2000 in Makuhari, Chiba (on the outskirts of Tokyo). At the time, one writer for the *Japan Times* saw tough times ahead for Daiei and other Japanese retailers.[11] The first store opening was closely followed about a month later by the second one on January 16, 2001 in Minami-Machida (Tokyo Metro area), which in turn was followed about a month later by the third Carrefour store opening in Myokohike in Izumi City—Daiei's back-yard in the Osaka area. Going forward, Carrefour's master plan through 2003 called for 10 more store openings throughout Japan.

This is not to suggest that Desvignes and Carrefour did not face struggles in Japan. Early sales fell short of estimates until the company brought in more Japanese managers and revamped aspects of the store to be a bit more Japanese. However, most aspects of the standard design of Carrefour stores were retained and were popular with Japanese consumers.[12] The Makuhari store had nearly 30,000 square meters of floor space, of which Carrefour directly managed and operated 17,014 square meters. The first floor of the Makuhari store, the area directly run and operated by Carrefour, included space for fresh foods, processed foods, daily goods, and a cafe-style food court. The second floor focused on clothing, home electrical appliances, and furniture. All told, there were over 60,000 items available (of which 7,000 were Carrefour-branded items)—making it one of Carrefour's largest and most diversified stores.

A total of 48 specialty shops occupied 7,535 square meters and included specialty clothing retailers that competed directly against Carrefour's own offering of clothing. But Desvignes believed that it was a big plus for consumers to be given the opportunity to make many choices. Some of the differentiators for Carrefour were its in-store bakery, chicken roasting station, and wide cheese selection. At the bakery, a special oven was imported from France, and the bread was baked and displayed for all to see. At the daily dish counter, 40 chickens on rotating skewers were cooked in a large-sized oven with huge glass doors. The cheese specialty shop offered dozens of kinds of cheeses from France and other parts of Europe. All this was a part of Carrefour's "theatrical production" used in designing the kitchen and counter areas in order to excite shoppers' appetites through "exhibition selling," in which Carrefour prepared foods right before customers' eyes and then sold them.

Carrefour's emphasis on low prices by dealing directly with manu-facturers was more difficult in Japan than in almost any other coun-try. Nevertheless, the Makuhari store reached a point at which 55% of its merchandise was sourced directly from manufacturers. For exam-ple, Carrefour dealt directly with Meiji Seika, a snack foods company, and received the popular chocolate stick snack "Fran" from the Meiji Seika distribution center in Saitama Prefecture that allowed Carrefour to sell it at a lower price than anywhere else in Japan.[13] However, many Japanese national brands that Carrefour carried were not cheaper at its Makuhari store compared with its Japanese competitors' stores.

After five years in Japan, in 2003, Desvignes and his family moved back to France. Desvignes joined Carrefour's M&A unit as the com-pany was accelerating its growth through the purchase of smaller retailers. In 2005 alone Carrefour acquired 12 hypermarkets in Poland; 160 mainly convenience stores in the Apulia region of Italy; 81 super-markets under the Gima brand in Turkey; 45 deep discount stores under the Endi brand in Turkey; 3 hypermarkets and 3 supermarkets under the Chris Cash&Carry brand in Cyprus; 10 hypermarkets from the Sonae Group in Sao Paolo, Brazil; 101 Penny Market stores under the Ed banner in France; 6 hypermarkets and 2 other projects from Tesco in Taiwan. In 2005, Carrefour also made modest divestitures in Mexico, France, Slovakia, the Czech Republic, and Spain.

One partial divestment that saddened Desvignes happened in Japan in 2005, two years after his departure from the country. In 2005, the senior management of Carrefour decided to move out of sole ownership in Japan and enter into a strategic partnership with Aeon (a large Japanese retailer). The press release from Carrefour read as follows:

Carrefour and Aeon have entered into a strategic partnership in Japan whereby:

- *Carrefour sells to Aeon its 8 hypermarkets, representing net sales of approx. € 326m*
- *The two parties enter into a partnership which covers (i) the use of the Carrefour brand in Japan, (ii) collaboration on selected commercial concepts and (iii) the sale of Carrefour private label products in Carrefour Japan stores (Aeon will also be able to sell labels such as "Reflets de France" in Aeon stores).*

The objective of Carrefour and Aeon is to develop and strengthen the hypermarket format in Japan through the alliance of the leading Japanese retailer and the second largest global retailer.[14]

Although overall Carrefour was successful and growing rapidly, it had specific stores and markets (such as Japan) in which it was struggling. As a consequence, in 2005 a new CEO as well as the Chairman was appointed of the Carrefour Group Management Board: José-Luis Durán, age 43.[15] The new CEO continued to press for growth through new store openings as well as acquisitions from 2005 through 2008. By 2008, Carrefour was #33 on the *Fortune Global 500* list; in contrast, Daiei had shrunk so much that it had fallen off the list two years earlier. By December 2007, Carrefour had nearly 15,000 stores worldwide.[16] It operated in more than 30 countries and received approximately 50% of its revenues from outside France. It had 1,163 hypermarkets, of which only 218 were in France. It had 6,166 hard discount stores, of which only 897 were in France. It operated 2,708 supermarkets, of which 1,021 were in France, and it ran 4,890 convenience and cash & carry stores, of which 3,379 were in France.

In November 2008, Desvignes heard that José Luis Durán was stepping down as CEO and being replaced by Lars Olofsson.[17] Olofsson was coming from Nestlé where he had held several key positions including Executive Vice President of the Nestlé Group with responsibility for all European activities. Olofsson was typical of the most senior executives in Nestlé. Even though he was working in a Swiss company, he was not Swiss but Swedish by passport. While he spoke his native Swedish, he was also fluent in English and French. While he loved his homeland, he had spent the majority of his professional career outside of it in France and Switzerland.

People speculated that the ousting of José Luis Durán and the official appointment of Lars Olofsson as the CEO on January 1, 2009 was due to the problem performance of Carrefour's business units inside France and the need to consolidate brands and offerings into a more coherent global position. Brand management and positioning was something that Nestlé did well, and Desvignes expected that Olofsson was recruited as CEO because he had these capabilities. This speculation was generally confirmed by Amaury de Sèze, Chairman of Carrefour's Board of Directors, when he declared:

> Lars Olofsson has exceptional experience in consumer markets, built over more than 30 years, both in France and internationally, within the number one global food industry group. His strong leadership and sales and marketing expertise make him the ideal leader for Carrefour to carry out the next stage of the Group's development.[18]

With Olofsson as the new CEO, 3 of the 10 members of the Executive Committee were now "foreigners" or non-French nationals. Desvignes believed this was further evidence that Carrefour was on a one-way journey to even greater globalization. While he saw great things under the previous CEO, he had even higher hopes for both future international expansion and more systematic global brand integration with the new CEO. As a consequence, when headhunters called on behalf of other firms such as Germany's Metro, the UK's Tesco, or the USA's Wal-Mart, it was fairly easy for Desvignes to listen politely but turn them down in the end. At nearly $100 billion in annual revenues in 2008, Carrefour was a distant second to the largest retailer in the world, Wal-Mart, which had nearly $400 billion in annual revenues. However, in Desvignes's mind, Wal-Mart, Metro, Tesco, and all the others were distant runners up to Carrefour in terms of global outlook and the development of international leaders.

FINAL COMMENTS

The real-life stories of Kenichi Tanaka and Jean-Louis Desvignes illustrate the challenges globalizing companies and individual managers face. Companies that move out of their home market comfort zones face challenges of cross-cultural management, leadership development, and growth. In many cases, Japanese companies *chose* to trade the challenges of cross-cultural management for the comfort of working from home and sending their products overseas. This tendency contributed to the decline in the standing of not just Daiei but a huge number of Japanese firms across all global industry sectors and segments.

In this chapter we wanted to highlight the human consequences and the individual career dynamics of these corporate decisions. While the future for Desvignes appears promising, Tanaka's future at Daiei is tentative at best. While much of what happened to Tanaka was out of his control, not all of it was. To some extent Tanaka's career advanced at Daiei because he fit in and made few waves. While deeply impacted by the results unfolding before him, he reacted somewhat passively to the mounting bad news and shortsighted decisions of his superiors. As a good "salaryman" Tanaka stoically suffered the consequences of Daiei's lack of effective globalization. While Desvignes has his own challenges to deal with going forward, most of us would choose his prospects over those of Tanaka.

Up to this point we have documented with data and illustrated with two case studies the consequences of Japanese MNCs lack of progress from the export to the regional and global stages of development. In the next three chapters we want to examine in more depth why and how this happened and discuss recommendations for the future.

9

THE INCREDIBLE SHRINKING JAPAN

At the outset of this book, we presented data that indicated Japanese firms were having a tough time in the global economy relative to firms from other countries. Recently, when we presented that data at a conference, a participant made the following comment and challenge:

Even if a global world is going to be tough for Japanese companies, why can't they continue to focus on Japan and still do well? After all Japan is the 2nd largest economy in the world. Plus, Japanese firms largely have the Japanese domestic market to themselves. So why do they need to think about and get so involved in the rest of the world's economy?

This is a fair question. Japan is not going to fall off the map in terms of being a big economy any time soon. Most of the forecasts we have seen show Japan gradually losing its ranking and sliding only to the #5 economy in the world after the United States, China, the European Union, and India by 2050. Falling from #2 to #5 is clearly not the end of the world. However, when you look into the details, it's not so much Japan's overall ranking as it is the country's relative growth or actual decline over the next 20 to 40 years that matters and should worry Japanese MNC executives.

Predicting economies 20 to 40 years in advance is tricky business. Just predicting the yen/dollar exchange rate 20 months from now is not easy. While economists get all excited about the details and nuances of econometric models and love nothing better than to debate esoteric statistical subtleties, our specialty is not economics. Furthermore, we doubt that most readers of this book are particularly interested in an in-depth overview of econometric modeling for Japan. As a consequence, we want to examine the key factors that play a role in a country's long-term economic prospects without getting tangled up in

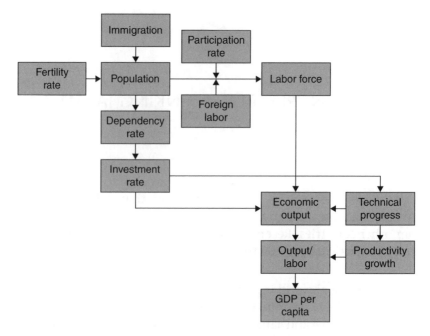

EXHIBIT 9.1 **Key Economic Factors**

technical details. In order to do this, let us first walk through a general model of these key factors that drive long-term economic prospects for a country and then come back to the key factors and fill in the numbers as they relate to Japan. Exhibit 9.1 provides a graphic illustration of the key factors we want to discuss and their general relationships.

Before we start reviewing this framework, we want to encourage you to have a page or two of patience as you read. As we said, the purpose of the next couple of pages is not to bore you or to turn you into an economist, but rather to systematically set the stage for you to understand why Japanese firms really cannot count on Japanese domestic economy as their salvation for the next 20 to 40 years and why they have no choice but to change and engage in the global economy or risk growing irrelevance. That said, let's dive in.

Fertility rate. It is fairly straightforward logic that all other things being equal, higher birth rates lead to a growing population. In addition, most people know that the required birth rate to keep a population constant is approximately 2.1.

Population. It is also fairly well understood that the total size of the population can have an important impact on the total size of the economy, though there are other factors that also come into play. Still, if you want to think about the economic prospects of a country, you have to consider its population prospects.

Immigration. The population of a country increases not only through more births but also through the arrival of new people who were born elsewhere—immigration. Conversely, the population of a country decreases if its citizens move to a different country—emigration.

Labor force. It stands to reason that in general the bigger the overall population, the more people you have in the labor force, working and producing economic outputs.

Participation rate. The total size of the labor force is not only affected by the size of the population but also by the proportion of the population that chooses to work. This is what economists call the participation rate in the labor force. Structural differences and cultural differences from country to country can affect the participation rate.

Foreign labor. The other major factor that can affect the total size of the labor force is foreign workers or people who have immigrated, not to become citizens, but to work. Obviously, a variety of factors can affect the size of the foreign labor pool including labor laws, cost of living, wages between the host and home country, etc. What we want to focus on is the outcome of these various factors, which is the size of the foreign labor pool.

Dependency rate. One of the other key issues relative to long-term economic prospects is the dependency ratio in the population. Most economists consider the dependency ratio as the proportion of the overall population that is 65 or older. This is relevant because in virtually all societies as people get older, they increasingly depend on younger people (family or otherwise) for economic support.

Investment rate. Dependency rates can, in turn, drive investment rates. As people get older, they shift the ratio of saving and consuming. As older people stop working or work less, their savings stop or decline, but their overall consumption remains more or less steady. As a consequence, the larger the portion of elderly people in a society, the lower the general savings rate, and therefore the lower the resulting investment rate. Investment rates, in turn, can clearly drive technology progress and overall output.

Technical progress. It is easy to understand why technical progress can affect overall economic output. Think of the output of people sewing clothes by hand, versus those using sewing machine, versus automated looms. Technical progress in turn is driven in part by investments. If you don't invest in developing automated looms, they tend not to be developed. Clearly, money is not the only thing that drives technical progress. Education, entrepreneurial incentives, cultural norms, etc. can all have an impact on technical progress. Yet, here again, we are not so interested in getting into all the detailed drivers of technical progress, as we are with its general outcome and its impact.

Economic output. If you are going to have growing standards of living, you generally need growing levels of output. A bigger labor force, greater investment, and higher technical progress can all contribute to higher economic output.

Productivity growth. To the individuals in a country it is not so much the overall economic output that affects their quality of life as it is the output per effective labor unit—that is, labor productivity.

Output per labor. As we noted, it is not just the overall output, but also the efficiency of that output that comes back to affect individual citizens and their standard of living.

GDP per capita. Finally, the quality of life for citizens is directly reflected by its GDP per capita.

LONG-TERM ECONOMIC PROSPECTS FOR JAPAN

In order to keep our discussion of Japan's long-term economic prospects from becoming too cumbersome, we need to mention a few things up front. First, as we already noted, predicting the future is a fool's game. Therefore, we are not going to try to precisely predict Japan's future GDP or GDP per capita but rather are going to articulate some facts from which we can speculate about the basic direction of Japan's economic future. Second, in painting a picture of Japan's future economic direction, we are going to present some data. In doing so, we know some readers will want more data than we provide and some will want less. If we don't hit the exact right balance for you personally, please accept our apologies in advance. Third, as the previous discussion showed, lots of interrelationships exist among the various factors. However, if we don't take a bit of a linear approach and touch on the factors one by one, it will get just too complicated. Finally, in order to help those who care about the overall conclusion but don't want to get into all the facts we present, we provide a summary of all the details (Exhibit 9.2) by reproducing the previous model and simply indicate by shading whether a particular factor is positive, neutral, or negative for the time periods 1950–2000 and 2001–2050.

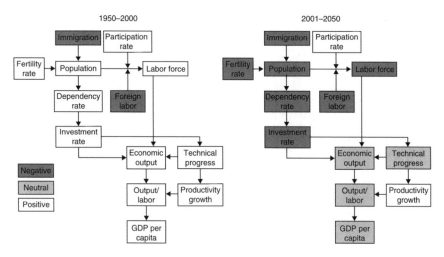

EXHIBIT 9.2 **Overview of Situation, 1950–2000 and 2001–2050**

While Exhibit 9.2 is a snapshot, many of the factors that we label as positive for Japan from 1950 to 2000 were actually less positive in 2000 compared to 1950. Conversely, many of the factors that we show as negative from 2001 to 2050 are more negative in 2050 than in 2001. It is important to note that even though a variety of factors are negative for the 2001–2050 period, the bottom line GDP-per-capita factor does not turn negative. But how can this be, given the number of driving factors that are labeled negative? The answer is simple. Japan has enough technological progress, investment, etc. to keep its GDP per capita growth from turning consistently negative. Nevertheless, we need to appreciate that the GDP per capita growth will change from very positive (and one of the fastest growth rates over the past 50 years), to neutral (and one of the slowest growth rates among all developed economies going into the next 50 years). If you're Japanese, this is not such great news. With all this as background, let's now walk through the individual elements and what their directional impact on Japan's long-term economic prospects seem to be.

Fertility rate

The fertility rate for Japan has dropped dramatically over the past nearly 60 years. It has declined from 3.65 in 1950 to 1.37 in 2007. As Exhibit 9.3 shows, this is even lower than many of the other developed economies in the world.

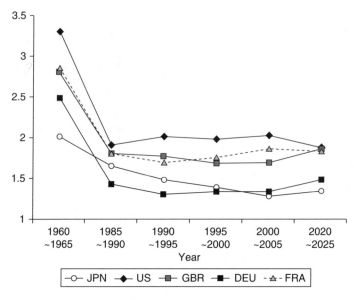

EXHIBIT 9.3 **Fertility Rates over Time**
Source: Japan Bureau of Statistics, 2008.

Population and immigration

While fertility rates can change, the change doesn't have an effect on the work force or the economy for almost 20 years. When looking into the future, this delayed relationship is great because by knowing the current fertility rate, we can project Japan's population out 20 years with some accuracy. The projection becomes much more reliable when you consider that the rate of immigration into Japan has been very low over the past 50 years. As we noted in Chapter 7, while the percentage of foreign-born residents increased from 0.5% of the population in 1950 to 1.5% by 2007, that still is significantly lower than most other developed economies. As a consequence, unless things change dramatically, Japan's population is projected to decrease from its peak in 2005 of 127 million to approximately 94 million in 2050—a 26% decline.[1]

Dependency ratio

However, it is not just the total size of the population but also its age composition that matters (see Exhibit 9.4).

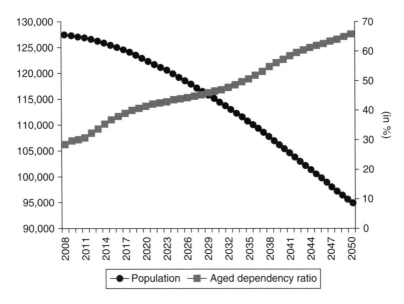

EXHIBIT 9.4 **Population Decline and Dependency Increase**
Source: Japan Bureau of Statistics, 2008.

In Japan's case, the dependency ratio is set to climb dramatically over the next 40 years. As we mentioned earlier, the higher the proportion of elderly people, the lower the overall investment rate. Fundamentally, in 1950 Japan had 10 workers for every person 65 or over. By 2008, that declined to 2.8 to 1, and by 2050 the ratio will decline even further to about 1.5 to 1. Exhibit 9.5 provides a more detailed visual of the change in the distribution of the population in Japan over time. As is easy to see, by 2050 the population pyramid will nearly have flipped upside down from where it was in 1950.

Investment rate

Older people not only work less and consume about as much but they also require more overall economic support. Whether this support comes from their families or from the government, the facts don't change. For example, the government of Japan estimates that the country's social security costs will go from ¥89.8 trillion in 2006 to ¥141 trillion by 2025 (a 57% increase) even though the total population will decline by 7%.[2] The Center for Economic Research in Japan estimates that the gross savings rate, which was 40% in 1970 and 28% in 2000, will decline to 17.4% by 2050.[3] As a consequence, relative to

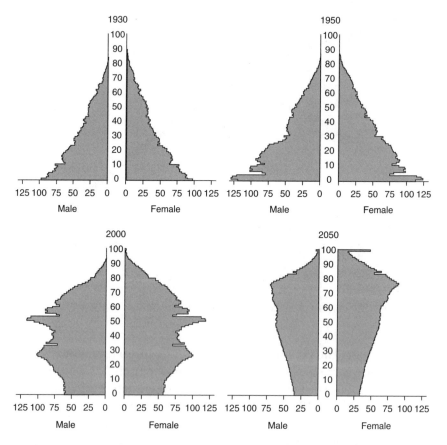

EXHIBIT 9.5 **Change in Population Distribution**
Source: National Institute of Population and Social Security Research.

the past, Japan will simply have less money to invest in technology, R&D, and other capital forming activities.

This could potentially be somewhat offset by foreign investment into Japan. However, the track record on this is not positive and as a result this doesn't seem very likely (Exhibit 9.6).

As we discussed earlier, the chart shows that Japan had one of the lowest FDI inflows as a percentage of GDP of any developed economy through the mid-1990s. This trend continued, and arguably accelerated, for the next decade.

As you examine the figures, you will notice some negative FDI inflows in certain years. People sometimes wonder how overall FDI inflows can be negative. It stems primarily from cases in which very little direct investment comes into a country and the foreign firm's

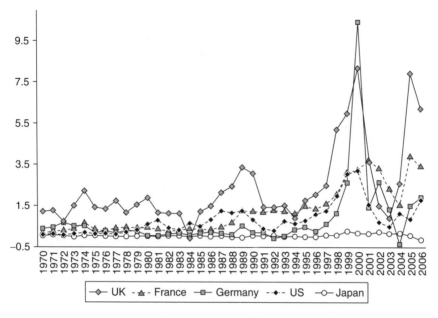

EXHIBIT 9.6 **FDI Inflows**
Source: UNTAD World Investment Report 2008.

retained earnings in the country are withdrawn and/or its assets in the country are divested. This is exactly what happened in 2006 when Vodafone withdrew from Japan and sold its business to Japan's Softbank for $15 billion. This single transaction was bigger than the other FDI inflows into Japan in 2006 and as a consequence, the total number for that year was negative.

Labor force, participation rate, and foreign workers

Given that the evidence is quite clear that Japan's population is going to decline, it's reasonable to assume that its overall work force will also decline. The only caveats would be if there are projected to be major increases in participation rates or influxes of foreign workers. Let's start with the last two moderating factors.

Foreign workers

A large influx of foreign workers just doesn't seem to be in the cards. As we already noted, for more than 50 years Japan has been very cautious about letting foreign workers into the country. In addition, the fact that foreigners would have to learn Japanese to function effectively puts many people at a disadvantage because of the large difference between the Japanese language and English and Romance languages such as French, Spanish, Italian, etc. The syntax of the Japanese language is most similar to Korean. This is partially why the largest group of foreigners in Japan are Koreans. In fact in 1950, Koreans constituted 91% of all foreigners in Japan. By 2006, this declined to 28.7%, but Koreans were still the largest single ethnic group in Japan with nearly 600,000 individuals in total. Chinese nationals constituted just 6.8% of all foreigners in 1950, but increased to 26.9% of the total and just over 561,000 individuals living in Japan by 2006. This increase is in part due to the common Chinese characters that are used in the written form of both languages.

The other notable group of foreigners in Japan are Brazilians, who constitute 15% of all foreigners in Japan. However, the overwhelming majority of these individuals are Brazilians by passport but Japanese by ethnicity. This stems from a group of over 164,000 Japanese who emigrated to Brazil between 1917 and 1940. This and subsequent groups of Japanese emigrants grew in Brazil until by 2006 they consisted of 1.4 million individuals and were the largest Japanese community outside of Japan. With the prosperity of Japan in the 1980s and a change in Japanese law, there was a dramatic increase in Japanese-Brazilians moving to Japan. Specifically, in 1988 there were 2,250 Brazilians living in Japan. By 1998, this increased to 222,217 individuals and continued to climb through 2006 when 313,969 individuals from Brazil were living in Japan.

In the end, while we see some increase in foreign workers in Japan, the increase is small and confined to three groups, and we see no dramatic increase in these three groups in the future. Given the prosperity of South Korea, it is hard to imagine a large influx of Koreans coming into Japan. Given the growth of Brazil and the relatively small base of Japanese-Brazilians in Brazil, it is also hard to imagine a significant increase from this group. Finally, although there is a very big group of Chinese who could be interested in coming to Japan, the growth and development of China and the relatively restrictive immigration and foreign worker regulations in Japan do not lead us to expect a significant increase in Chinese foreign workers going forward.

Participation rate

As we mentioned, the total size of the labor force can be affected by the participation rate. Japanese men on average have a higher participation rate than the men in other developed countries, especially in the older age brackets as is illustrated in Exhibit 9.7. As a consequence, a higher participation rate in the future from Japanese men is highly unlikely, and therefore all other things being equal a decline in the male working age population will translate into a decrease in the overall workforce.

In Japan, as in most countries, women participate at a lower rate than men. However, Japanese women participate at a lower rate than women in many other developed countries, except in the older age brackets where Japanese women (like Japanese men) have generally a higher participation rate than older women in many other developed countries (see Exhibit 9.8). As a consequence, there is room for some higher levels of female participation, especially in the 30–45 age range. However, even if Japanese women in the 30–45 age range participated at a rate comparable to women in other developed countries, by 2030 the weighted average improvement (about 14%) would increase the overall labor force by only 4%, and Japan would still see its labor force decline from just over 67 million in 2006 to approximately 61 million in 2030 and decline further to 44 million by 2050—a drop of nearly 70%!

As these exhibits illustrate, higher participation rates by Japanese men are highly unlikely in the future and higher participation rates from women would likely do little to offset the negative impact of a declining population on a declining workforce.

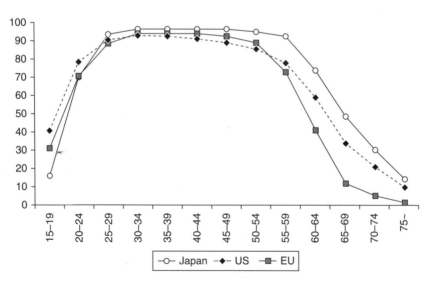

EXHIBIT 9.7 **Male Labor Participation Rates**
Source: Japan Bureau of Statistics, 2008.

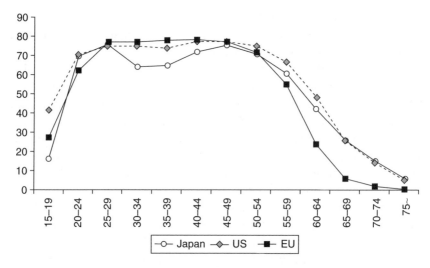

EXHIBIT 9.8 **Female Labor Participation Rates**
Source: Japan Bureau of Statistics, 2008.

Technical progress and productivity

Academics can get twisted up into all sorts of intellectual knots with various estimations, adjustments, bias corrections, and the like when it comes to the topics of technological progress, productivity, and what is typically called "total factor productivity" (TFP). Fortunately for our purposes, we do not need to worry about these technical issues. This is because while disagreements exist over the exact numbers, there is reasonable agreement across multiple studies about the direction of TFP changes in Japan. In manufacturing industries such as automotive, Japan has made fairly good use of its invested capital in being more productive, though the rate of improvement has declined over the past 40 years. In contrast to manufacturing, Japan's productive use of capital in service industries, such as retailing and wholesaling and in agriculture, have not helped, and during some periods of time have even hurt, Japan's overall TFP.

Some of the most widely cited figures are those by Professor Dale Jorgenson of Harvard and Professor Koji Nomura of Keio University (see Exhibit 9.9).[4]

Exhibit 9.9 shows how overall TFP growth has declined in Japan since 1960 but has actually increased in the United States. It also shows that early on, non-IT capital input made an important contribution in Japan and continued to be positive but diminished over time. IT capital input in the United States has had a growing impact while in Japan it

EXHIBIT 9.9 **Total Factor Productivity Growth in Japan and the United States**

	1960–1973	1973–1990	1990–1995	1995–2000	2000–2004	1960–2004
United States						
Value added	3.90	2.83	2.35	4.12	2.56	3.21
Capital input	1.81	1.59	1.19	2.14	1.46	1.66
IT capital	0.21	0.41	0.49	0.97	0.63	0.44
Non-IT capital	1.60	1.18	0.70	1.16	0.83	1.22
Labor input	1.29	1.08	0.81	1.29	−0.17	1.02
Total factor productivity	0.81	0.17	0.35	0.69	1.27	0.54
Agriculture	0.00	0.13	0.03	0.07	0.10	0.07
IT-manufacturing	0.09	0.20	0.27	0.48	0.04	0.19
Motor vehicle	0.02	0.00	−0.01	0.02	0.06	0.01
Other manufacturing	0.52	−0.02	0.11	0.21	0.04	0.19
Communication	0.01	0.06	−0.01	−0.04	0.07	0.03
Trade	0.17	0.15	0.07	0.15	0.51	0.18
Finance & insurance	−0.05	0.01	0.04	0.11	0.30	0.03
Other services	0.04	−0.37	−0.14	−0.30	0.15	−0.17
Japan						
Value added	10.00	4.50	1.31	1.31	1.14	5.10
Capital input	4.95	2.19	1.93	1.02	0.72	2.71
IT capital	0.22	0.26	0.27	0.32	0.37	0.27
Non-IT capital	4.72	1.93	1.66	0.70	0.35	2.44
Labor input	1.75	1.12	−0.16	−0.19	−0.15	0.90
Total factor productivity	3.30	1.18	−0.46	0.48	0.57	1.48
Agriculture	0.20	0.00	0.06	−0.01	−0.04	0.06
IT manufacturing	0.17	0.21	0.09	0.42	0.35	0.22
Motor vehicle	0.28	0.13	0.00	0.02	0.11	0.14
Other manufacturing	1.78	0.41	−0.33	0.17	0.08	0.68
Communication	0.07	0.05	0.07	0.12	0.08	0.07
Trade	0.94	0.28	0.01	−0.13	−0.03	0.37
Finance & insurance	0.23	0.10	−0.22	0.15	0.04	0.10
Other services	−0.36	0.01	−0.14	−0.26	−0.03	−0.15

Note: All figures are average annual growth rates. Value added is aggregated from industry GDPs evaluated at the factor of cost.
Source: The Industry Origins of the US-Japan Productivity Gap, Dale Jorgenson and Koji Nomura, Japan Project Meeting, June 26–27, 2007, Tokyo, Japan.

has remained positive though at a lower level. Motor vehicle contribution to TFP has been positive and steady in Japan but low in the United States. In contrast, while improvements in other services in the United States have increased, they have generally been declining in Japan over the past 45 years with only one period of minor improvement.

Long-term economic prospects

So what will Japan's GDP or GDP per capita be by 2050? The only safe answer is to say, "No one knows for sure." Anyone who had a crystal ball and could predict a given country's economic performance 10, 20, let alone 40 years in advance would be insanely rich and world famous. That said, the evidence does allow us to point to the likely economic prospects for Japan over the next 40 years. It is clear that Japan's economic prospects over the next 40 years look much worse than those of the previous 40 years. This is because it seems an almost certainty that Japan's population will decline by about 25% to 30% and its workforce will decline by about 60% to 70% over the next 40 years. Its number of citizens 65 and older will more than double and balloon to nearly 40% of the total population. As a consequence, Japan will increasingly need to spend more money and energy supporting these older folks. In doing so, the country will have less money to invest and to make up its decline in labor with productivity improvements from capital. Furthermore, if the past 40 years are any indication, the prospect of productivity improvements from capital in key sectors of the economy such as agriculture, retail, wholesale, and other services looks dim, not bright. Given the general economic movement of Japan and all industrialized countries from manufacturing to service sectors, this lack of service-sector productivity will be particularly problematic for Japan. Perhaps liberalization and/or the devaluation of the yen will attract foreign firms in, which have much higher levels of productivity in service sectors, and they will help boost Japan's service sector productivity. This is possible, but given 40 years of low levels of immigration, strict rules that allow few foreign workers in, and low FDI inflows, this prospect also looks dim, not bright.

These factors are why respected institutions such as the Economic Research Group (ERG) in Japan and the Japan Center for Economic Research (JCER) have dim rather than bright estimates for Japan's future (see Exhibit 9.10 in which the estimates come primarily from JCER but ERG estimates are noted in [] brackets).

EXHIBIT 9.10 **Growth Estimates**

GDP Growth	1990–2000	2001–2010	2011–2020	2021–2030	2031–2040	2041–2050
Japan	1.2	1.2 [1.4]	1.4 [0.6]	1.0 [0.3]	0.6 [−0.3]	0.0 [−0.4]
US	3.1	2.9	2.8	2.5	2.4	2.3
EU	2.4	1.7	1.8	1.2	1.1	0.9
GDP per Capita Growth						
Japan	0.9	1.0	1.6	1.7	1.5	1.1
US	2.0	2.0	1.9	1.8	1.9	1.8
EU	2.1	1.4	1.7	1.3	1.3	1.3
GDP per Labor Growth						
Japan	0.6	1.5 [1.4]	1.7 [1.2]	1.8 [1.0]	1.9 [0.8]	1.5 [0.7]
US	1.9	1.9	2.1	2.0	1.9	1.9
EU	2.0	1.1	1.8	1.9	1.7	1.6
ERG Estimates						
TFP	0.8	0.7	0.3	0.1	−0.2	−0.3
Gross Savings	27.7	25.3	22.5	21.6	19.2	17.4
Net Savings	8.7	3.8	0.0	−0.8	−2.4	−3.0

Sources: Tatsuya Ishikawa, *Population Decrease, Aging, and Japan's Long-Term Economic Outlook to 2050,* Economic Research Group, 2002; *Demographic Change and the Asian Economy,* Japan Center for Economic Research, 2002.

As we said, no one can precisely predict the future 20 or 40 years from now, but the estimates in Exhibit 9.10 are sobering. The good news is that if you are a Japanese citizen, all of the factors we have covered do not necessarily mean that your standard of living will decline. In fact, estimates of GDP growth per capita and GDP growth per employed person will be low but will remain positive. In contrast, if you are a Japanese company primarily focused on the domestic market, the "go-go growth" days of the 1960s, 70s, 80s, and even 1990s are going…going…gone! If you want to continue to grow, you have no choice but to turn your focus outside Japan.

CONCLUSION

In closing this chapter, we want to be clear about two things. First, we are *not* saying that even if these general projections are correct that there is no opportunity for certain Japanese firms to grow successfully with a Japan-domestic market focus. Clearly, care for elderly in general, healthcare, medicine, and other related areas are going to be growth sectors in Japan going forward. Japan will have one of the largest elderly populations in absolute terms (not just in relative terms) in the world. There will undoubtedly be money-making and business growth opportunities in this broad sector. There may be other sectors of growth that no one can even anticipate now. For example, if Japan emerges as the center of the world for cold fusion or nano technology, Japanese firms in those areas will grow.

What we are saying is that across the broad spectrum of sectors and industries, Japanese MNCs that try to continue a domestically focused strategy are likely to fall farther behind their MNC competitors that are taking a more global perspective and approach. What is cause for concern is that none of what we have presented in this chapter is new to Japanese government officials, farsighted Japanese executives, or academics. In fact, we have been a part of some of these high-level conversations in Japan for years. Yet, the stagnation of the "lost decade," which now seems as though it will surely turn into the "lost generation," suggests a "deer caught in the headlights" phenomenon.

It reminds us of a recent interaction that one of the authors had with an old high school buddy Joe (real person but disguised name). In talking with Joe, he was eager to relive and talk about his glory days of high school when he was king of the campus. You could hear in his voice and see in his eye how much he longed for those "yester years." Of course, his high school campus consisted of just a few hundred students who came from the surrounding town of a few thousand people. As a consequence, it is no surprise that Joe played in three sports and was the captain of the baseball team and was class president. However, when Joe faced the challenge of going to university where 30,000 students came from all over the country and other parts of the world, he froze. He could not go back and he was afraid to move forward. So Joe stood still, or so he thought. But as Joe stood still, the rest of the world marched on and left Joe behind. In relative terms, even though Joe thought he was standing in place, he was actually sliding backwards.

Sadly, Japanese companies cannot go back in time and reclaim the factors that put the wind at their backs. Those days are gone. In fact, our contention is that the favorable domestic and export winds of the past have not just died down but they have also shifted and turned into headwinds for Japanese firms sailing into a global future. Consequently, Japanese firms and Japanese executives have to make some major changes if they are going to continue to grow and be relevant in the global future. In the next chapter, we outline what we see as some of those needed changes.

10

SO WHAT ARE THE JAPANESE TO DO?

By now it should be apparent that Japanese MNCs are in a heap of trouble. A model for success, that if not invented by the Japanese was perfected by them, has grown stale. The external environment and Japan's own internal demographics have changed. The "Made in Japan" brand has slipped as Toyota will attest. Japanese companies have fallen behind. The world is moved on.

So what should Japanese MNC executives do to turn the tide and get back their mojo? To be honest, we are a little nervous answering this question and making recommendations to Japanese executives. Why? Because even if you believe you have correct advice to offer, if you don't believe that advice has a good chance of being implemented, you wonder if it is really going to change anything. From a practical perspective, good advice needs to be both directionally correct and realistically feasible. What advice would you offer a wheezing, coughing chain smoker? Stop smoking. Fine, but what's the likelihood of change? Maybe not so great. Similarly, what advice would you offer a young worker, in a dead-end job? Quit, and go work for someone else. Sounds good, but what if the worker is a risk-averse, sole bread-winner for a young family? He is more likely to stay put than to put it all at risk. Objective advice and practical advice are often at odds.

The bottom line for us is that we want to provide recommendations that based on our analysis are directionally correct but also, based on our interactions and interviews with scores of Japanese executives, have a chance of being put into practice, at least by those executives who are motivated and determined not to be left further behind.[1] To those Japanese executives who say as *gaijin* (outsiders) we don't understand Japan and that things can only change gradually, we say, "The data don't lie."

That said, we offer recommendations to two constituencies. First we have recommendations to the senior managers of Japanese companies—those decision makers who are charged with determining

strategy and setting company policy. Second, we have recommendations to individual employees—at all level—of Japanese companies. To
this group, our advice is geared particularly to those who are prepared
to take charge of their own development and if necessary are ready to
act independently of their companies.

PART I: RECOMMENDATIONS FOR SENIOR JAPANESE EXECUTIVES

We all must face the facts. The Japanese stock market has dropped
more than 80% from its high in 1989. The standing of Japanese MNCs
in the *Fortune Global 500* has fallen by 50% since 1995. MNCs from
developing countries, such as Korea and China, are pushing past some
of the premier Japanese brand names of yesteryear. Significant growth
focused on the Japanese domestic market looks doubtful as far as the
eye can see.

As a consequence, there is no substitute for decisive leadership—
leaders who are prepared to make significant and needed changes. The
good news is that not since the end of World War II have Japanese
employees been so hungry for and in need of clear direction and decisive leadership. To those leaders we offer some pointed advice.

Become acutely aware of your own cognitive biases

All of us, Japanese, American, Russian, French, etc., are bound up in
our thinking by past paradigms. These mental maps influence what we
think we see, how we interpret it, and what we do as a consequence.[2]
For a long time, people thought the sun rotated around the earth and
that the world was flat. Thinking the world was flat kept people from
sailing too far from shore. People hung on to this mental map not
because they were stupid but because it worked. Not sailing far from
the sight of shore kept many ships from sinking and many sailors from
dying in violent, deep ocean storms.

Consider, for example, that 250 years ago *Encyclopedia Britannica*
invented the entire notion of an encyclopedia. The original one
was a bound, three-volume set. As the knowledge contained in the
Encyclopedia Britannica expanded, so did the number of bound volumes.
This paradigm of capturing and selling knowledge in bound books
worked spectacularly well for more than 235 years. When it came to

106

encyclopedias, *Britannica* was the company. However, when first CDs and then the Internet came along, executives could not break free of their past success and mental maps. As a consequence, *Encyclopedia Britannica* eventually saw 80% of its sales disappear—never to return unless and until executives update their maps to where the world of knowledge is now and where it is going tomorrow.

Japanese executives have exactly the same challenge. As an example, focusing on the Japanese domestic market and exporting to the world worked spectacularly well for decades. Sadly, the weather changed and all the favorable winds that helped Japan during that period have either died away or turned into headwinds. And yet, it seems many Japanese executives have almost instinctively, reflectively turned back to what worked before. Recall that we noted earlier that exports as a percentage of GDP grew and in 1984 peaked at 13.9%. Over the next 10 years, the percentage declined until reaching a bottom in 1994 of 8.0%. As the headwinds of the "lost generation" blew against Japanese executives, they turned back to their old playbook and again cranked up exports. As a percentage of GDP, exports climbed from 8.0% in 1994 to 12.4% in 2004 and to an all-time record high of 18.6% in 2007! The export model and miracle seemed to be working again, until the *tsunami* wave of the economic crisis of 2008 and 2009 rolled up the shores of Japan. As consumers around the world put away their wallets for Japanese exports, Japan saw an annualized GDP decline of 12.7% in the fourth quarter of 2008—its largest economic decline in nearly 40 years! Perhaps the lessons are not being learned.

Whatever the paradigm, we have to keep in mind that your mental map is there for one reason and one reason alone—it worked in the past. The more successful it was in the past and the longer it worked, the harder it is to change. As a consequence, the more vulnerable we are if it becomes outdated. Therefore, one of the best things any executive can do, and our first point of advice if you are a Japanese executive, is to identify those mental maps or those automatic, instinctive, reflexive responses that you have built up over a successful career. For example, when foreign executives quit, do you reflexively think that it just proves that foreigners can't be trusted and can't become global executives in a Japanese company? You may be right in your judgment or you may be dead wrong. Recognize that the more automatic, instinctive, reflexive your response, the more likely your mental map ought to be examined preemptively and proactively. No one wants to be the last executive standing at *Encyclopedia Britannica* as it files for bankruptcy because he was sure that if the books were bound just a little nicer, if the binding costs were squeezed just a bit tighter, the sinking ship could be righted.

The problem for people "in-side" a paradigm is that it is nearly impossible to see outside of it. You can become blinded by your own experiences and limited if too many people around you also have similar experiences and mental maps. This is why in addition to trying to personally reflect on your paradigms and mental maps, we quickly come to our second recommendation: race to add diversity.

Race to add diversity

While cognitive awareness is a necessary step, the more deeply engrained the paradigms, the more likely you cannot break them on your own. You have to add people who are not like you. Diversity helps break down paradigms and allows decision makers to become more aware of their own mental models.

By now in the book, it should be amply clear that Japanese companies are generally less culturally diverse than companies from the United States and the Europen Union. What can be done about this? To us, the clarion call to "hire more foreigners" rings hollow. First, who, among the most talented of the world, would want to quit their current high-powered jobs to go work for one of the big Japanese MNCs? When they arrive, they can't speak to their colleagues, they are largely ostracized, and their careers are capped. So attracting and integrating these folks is going to be very tough. So what can be done, in practical terms? We offer some "creative" suggestions below.

Use international joint ventures more creatively

As any company grows, it faces a variety of strategic alternatives: internal development, mergers and acquisitions, and JVs are the most common. In terms of developing more diversity amongst the management ranks, joint ventures have a wide number of benefits:

- Because they are joint ventures and not takeovers, there is far less risk of destroying the prevailing culture of the partner company. This will increase the likelihood that talent from the partner's side will stay in place and not look for the exit.
- These in-house sources of talent can be tested for leadership quality as well as their cultural skills. In some circumstances, they represent

a source for future recruits. However, most likely their influence can have positive benefits for resident Japanese managers. The Japanese managers who are seconded to the JV will come under intense pressure to adjust their approaches to business as well as their values. Over time, the impact on them, on the JV, and on the parent company can be profound.

- JVs represent talent breeding grounds. Japanese companies can send their employees to the JV for short-term stints designed to learn best practices, develop a broader perspective of other markets, cultures, management approaches, etc.
- Joint ventures present options for future acquisitions, without requiring large up-front commitments of time and resources.
- The joint ventures themselves can be scaled up or down depending on market conditions. In growth scenarios, the JV can be expanded. This in turn translates into a diminishing reliance on Japanese managers in the corporation's overall value creation model.
- In tougher times, the JV can be wound up, with limited risk to the parent company.

We are encouraged by the recent moves of some Japanese companies to shift increasingly to joint ventures as part of their globalization efforts. However, we wonder whether the "people development" potential of these structures is fully understood. For example, in early April 2009, Sharp announced plans to shift its core production from Japan. Sharp is one of Japan's biggest manufacturers and one of the few consumer electronics companies in that country to continue manufacturing its own LCD panels. Others are mere assemblers, buying components from China or Korea. Faced with mounting competition from the likes of LG, Samsung, and numerous Taiwanese and Chinese competitors, Sharp made the decision to shift production out of Japan. According to Sharp's President, Mikio Katayama, "exports from Japan will not make sense even in the most advanced technological fields."[3]

Sharp's strategy is primarily designed to reduce exposure to the fluctuations of the yen as well as to lower up-front investment costs. In a blow to the company's ability to fully control overseas operations, the strategy calls for the extensive reliance on overseas partners, with Sharp taking only minority equity interests. Sharp's joint venture with Enel, Italy's largest energy company, to produce solar panels for Europe serves as a role model for the company's future globalization efforts. To the extent possible in this type of situation we have seen great benefits when individuals from the partners have been brought into

Japan and when Japanese managers have been sent out into the joint ventures explicitly for development purposes and not just to apply technical capabilities. In Sharp's case it is not entirely clear if these sorts of indirect paths to diversity and its benefits have been fully explored and incorporated into the strategic plans.

Use M&As wisely

M&As offer a quick approach to broadening the ranks of non-Japanese management. If you can't build them from within or if there are strategic limits on your potential to benefit from JVs, then the logical next best option is to buy a solution to your human capital problem. And by global standards there are a lot of rich Japanese companies that have been waiting too long on the sidelines to do just this. But how should you best structure these deals, particularly if you are concerned about broadening the ranks of management in the company *overall*?

The three most common post-acquisition strategies include (1) stand-alone acquisitions, (2) absorbed acquisitions, and (3) best-of-both mergers.[4] Best-of-both mergers have the appeal of taking what is good in both companies and blending them. Both companies change and in essence a new company is formed in the process. Best-of-both mergers have the added appeal of being relatively easy to sell, particularly to shareholders and top employees. After all, mergers are a lot less threatening than whole-sale acquisitions. So one approach to globalization in general and globalizing Japanese management more specifically would be to use best-of-both mergers liberally.

A good example of a successful best-of-both merger involves Nippon Sheet Glass and Pilkington of the United Kingdom. Founded in Osaka in 1918 as American Japan Sheet Glass, the company got its start by importing valuable glass making technology from US-based Libby Owens Ford Glass. In 1931, the company officially changed its name to Nippon Sheet Glass (NSG). After World War II, NSG grew in Japan and then went on a buying binge, gobbling up Nippon Safety Glass, Nippon Glass Fiber, Micro Optics, and Nippon Muki Company. In 2004, it moved its head office to Tokyo.

Pilkington was one of NSG's major competitors. In 1986, it had purchased Libbey Owens Ford, NSG's original supplier of technology. With a strong domestic position but weak presence overseas and worried about losing its technological edge, NSG purchased 20% of Pilkington in 2001. Five years later, they purchased the remaining 80% they did not own. The purchase effectively doubled NSG's size and gave it manufacturing operations in 29 continents and sales in 130 countries. The post-acquisition strategy was clearly "best of both." By working together, NSG and Pilkington could improve production efficiencies, better underwrite technology investments, and improve penetration of particularly emerging markets. The new Group would generate only 27% of its sales in Japan. As a sign of the seriousness of their commitment to best of both, the NSG Group appointed Stuart Chambers as its president (formerly the CEO of Pilkington Stuart Chambers). This was the first non-Japanese president NSG employees had known. Of the 35 senior executives of the company, 17 were non-Japanese nationals.

While it is still early days, the actions of the NSG Group have certainly gotten the attention of other Japanese MNCs. It is admittedly difficult to tease apart the financial results and imagine the financial performances if the two companies had not merged, but in the midst of a tough recession NSG Group remains profitable. In January 2009, faced with declining sales in its automotive and building products businesses, NSG Group announced a significant restructuring initiative including plant closures and layoffs impacting 15% of the company's global workforce. Its aggressive efforts showed positive results and its stock price gained over 11% in just the last 6 months of 2009.

Best-of-both mergers are tough to pull off even in the best of times. They promise diversity, market access, and an immediate bump in sales and profits, but are tricky to implement. As a result, we argue for caution in taking this approach because best-of-both mergers are fraught with difficulty, even within the same culture, let alone cross-culturally. Who makes decisions when you have to decide "best-of-both?" What happens to customers during the years it takes to integrate cultures? What are the consequences for employee morale and trust when building the new organization drags on and on? In the case of NSG, they were smart in diversifying the ranks of their top executives. But getting 17 non-Japanese to work with 18 Japanese peers is a huge challenge that won't quickly go away. Unless the leadership team is committed to making it work and until they receive loads of cross-cultural and communications training, taking a best-of-both approach to M&As is a formula for customer alienation and talent flight.

And yet if the objective is increasing diversity overall, M&As can play a central role. Our advice is that executives interested in broadening and *retaining* international talent should consider the stand-alone acquisition option as their first choice. To be used to their best effect, Japanese companies pursuing stand-alone acquisitions would get the most mileage if these were made in non-competing industry sectors. They could be established as options on future uncertainties, scaling them up or down depending on opportunities. Because the parent company would have little or no experience in the "new" industry, its ability to add value through "tinkering" would be severely limited, thus reducing the temptation to absorb and smother the new venture. By leaving the acquisition alone, the existing management would be less likely to leave and more open to using the venture to incubate new ideas and new leaders.

Because acquisitions usually command a premium price, a stand-alone venture becomes an expensive option. It would only make sense if the acquisition met the dual imperatives of corporate diversification *and* leadership diversification.

Revise the policy for promotion

In a huge number of global companies like Nestlé of Switzerland, Akzo Nobel of The Netherlands, Daimler of Germany, Nokia of Finland, and Aramco of Saudi Arabia, English has become the language of senior management. These are all highly successful companies that depend on global talent for their success. Each is based outside an English-speaking country but has decided to require English language skills of its senior managers. In the case of Nestlé, fluency in three languages is now a requirement for executive advancement. These policies have gone beyond debate and have become imbedded in the culture and values of the organization.

Critical to the success of Japanese companies in attracting global talent and connecting with customers overseas is breaking the language barrier. And yet with few exceptions, the language abilities of top managers at Japanese companies are mixed at best. Fluency means different things to different people, but assessments of English skills are often inflated in Japanese companies. We have witnessed this first-hand in executive programs we have run. In one example, all 20-odd Japanese participants in the program were certified as fluent in English. We wondered, however, how accurate this assessment was when they all showed up with electronic dictionaries and with communications skills that were, with few exceptions, embarrassingly weak.

For those who work closely with senior managers from many compa-nies, the Japanese are often singled out for their weak English language skills. This is particularly problematic for a country with a population of less than 130 million, and shrinking. Continued global relevance is just not possible without significantly strengthening the English language skills of particularly the top management. Our advice: make true fluency a pre-requisite for advancement to the top rungs of the company!

We are beginning to see small cracks in the traditional approaches to succession management at Japanese companies. Much has been written about dramatic effect CEO Carlos Ghosn has had on the company's fortunes, both at home and abroad since his appointment as CEO in June 2001. Ghosn is one of only a few foreigners at the helm of Japanese companies. Even so, Ghosn's time is split between his co-CEO responsibilities at Nissan and Renault. Sir Howard Stringer, the British-American CEO of Sony is another notable example. Appointed in June 2005 as Sony's Chairman and CEO, Stringer has been credited with restructuring Sony and of making it more responsive to global consumers, faster and less Japan-centric in its culture and approach.

A major obstacle to expanding the number of non-Japanese, "global" CEOs is the governance structure of many Japanese companies. In virtually all US and European companies an external or advisory board, comprised of many outside or independent directors, supervises the CEO. In Japan, boards are most commonly filled with senior staff, company bankers, or representatives of trading partners. This discourages the hiring of people outside the "loop" or those who might be prone to "radical" thinking.[5] At a minimum, it seems that Japanese firms also need to add representatives to their board who are executives at other Japanese companies but not part of the traditional *keiretsu* network.

Pour resources in developing global leaders

After all is said and done, the only thing that will save Japanese companies from the setting sun is leadership. This has to be the starting point. Global leaders are those who not only "see things as they really are" both inside and outside the company, but they also have the skills to attract the right talent to their teams, irrespective of country of origin. They have the ability to marshal and channel company resources to solving problems and capitalizing on opportunities in the marketplace. In doing so, global leaders build an organization, including the culture and supporting mechanisms, that becomes self-sustaining in its ability to execute quickly and adapt to fast changing market conditions.

Investing in people is hugely important for all companies, but particularly so for the Japanese. Increasingly, all companies have access to the same or comparable technologies. Factor cost differentials are also fast disappearing in many industries. And with the labor component of many Japanese manufacturers now representing less than 8% of total costs, knowledge workers will increasingly determine the competitiveness of companies.[6] The quality of the management—their ability to recognize global opportunities for growth, capitalize on and build firm-specific global resources, and build and effectively use cross-cultural teams—will differentiate the successful Japanese companies of the 21st century from the losers.

While it is easy to recommend developing global leaders, how can this be done? What are the steps that Japanese companies should take to accelerate the global leadership development process? While entire books have been written on this topic,[7] we offer a few highlights for consideration.

Define what good looks like

If you want to build a house, you first have to be clear on what you want it to look like. Do you want it to be an Asian style, Swiss Chalet, or Colorado Ranch? What functions do you want it to serve? Lots of entertaining? Family only? Where should the house be positioned on the lot or land? This only makes sense. Similarly, if you want to build more global leaders, you have to spend time defining what good looks like. Ideally, this process would identify competencies and values that are at the heart of success going forward.

The last people to involve in this process would be the existing executives. Their skills got them to where they are today. They are masters at the *old* system. While they may have some interesting ideas on what it will take to succeed in the future, the reality is that they will be retired for a long time before the skills of the next generation of leaders become truly valued. No, it is better to look at the leadership needs and competencies required in the future to define what good looks like. This review and definition process should involve HR professionals and thought leaders in the broader HR community. Going forward, it should also include broad and deep discussions with the company's strategy community to better understand the direction of company, the timing of key moves, and the competencies needed.

Develop corporate people systems

While every company organizes its people or human resource management systems differently, we usually think of six major functions as being critical: (1) recruitment, (2) employee engagement and retention, (3) identifying and developing high potential employees, (4) performance management (5) succession management, and (6) training and development. While some aspects of each of these functions will necessarily have a local component, most Japanese companies lack a coherent model for globalizing their people management. Far too often, corporate HR plays a support role and exists to gather data and prepare reports. HR is viewed as far too tactical and operational and anything but a strategic partner. This has to change if Japanese companies are ever to effectively tackle the challenges of globalization.

Entire books could be written on how companies could globalize each of the six major people/HR management functions. Key to all of this is recognizing that not *all* supporting practices should be globalized. Rather, consistent with embracing a true borderless global model, the people "solution" for Japanese companies will require a mixture of local, regional, and global approaches. A global competency model will require some regional adaptations as well as local performance assessments. The real challenge for corporate people/HR executives is to develop within their organizations the capabilities and sophistication to pull off this complex task consistently and with the respect and support of the business lines.

PART II: ADVICE TO THE INDIVIDUAL JAPANESE MANAGER

If you are a Japanese executive and have gotten this far in the book, you have no doubt uncovered lessons that are idiosyncratic to you and your situation. Hopefully, you have begun to reassess where you are at in terms of your own skills, interests, and career opportunities. You have also begun to more effectively size up your company in order to determine its overall strengths and weaknesses as well as its potential for you to have an interesting career and rewarding life overall.

We want to encourage you to think about your overall interests in a more critical way. You are not trapped, unless you allow yourself to take this position. You are free to decide if you want to play a part in a global, even borderless company and if so, what this role might be. You are free to determine where your opportunities are the greatest and to what degree you should be bound by loyalties, fears, and risk avoidance. Clearly, these decisions have inevitable trade-offs. In thinking through these challenges, we offer three questions that can help:

1. Does your company provide you the global development opportunities you desire?
2. To what degree do you want to lead change versus follow others who take on a global leadership role?
3. If you want to play a leadership role, to what degree can you make the kinds of changes needed to create an environment that will allow you and the people you care most about to flourish?

For some, the answer to these questions will come easily: my current company provides everything I need or provides me enough of what I want, given the sacrifices I am prepared to make. For others, the answer will be more nuanced and end with "I am not sure what to think. I'll wait for more clarity. I will wait for someone else to help me sort it out and tell me what to do." And still for others the answer is "I am unhappy. I am not growing. I am not having fun. I need to find another kind of organization." It is to this last group of people that we offer a few additional suggestions.

Take charge of your own development

Don't wait for your boss or HR manager to tap you on the shoulder and offer you a great development opportunity. You will likely wait a long time. Take the initiative yourself. Ask for developmental assignments outside Japan, preferably in developed countries where you will more likely be exposed to leading-edge business practices. Attend executive development programs, ideally spending at least two weeks per year outside Japan in courses. Work on your English. Build your technical skills. Volunteer to lead global committees or join multicountry task forces.

Build your network

Recognize that good managerial jobs most often come through networks that extend beyond the footprint of your company, its suppliers, and customers. Build your Rolodex to include professionals outside Japan and far removed from your company. A good place to start is by joining professional groups, or through executive education programs. Spend time every day, reconnecting with people outside your in-company network. Talk to head-hunters. Talk to former classmates with whom you went to school.

Take the plunge

While never easy, particularly if you are used to lifetime employment, the time will certainly come when your ambitions for a more global career will become stymied at home. If and when the time is right, take the plunge. For most people who have succeeded in making this move, taking a job with a non-Japanese firm has eased the transition.

Lead while you can

The ability to change things is often at its highest when you are new to an organization. You arrive with new ideas and new energy. And you don't know enough to NOT want to lead. These early days are critical for you to develop a constituency, to organize your team, and to make a lasting difference.

While it would be tempting to think that if you are restless you have to find another organization, you don't always have to leave to do this. In many cases, you can lead from where you are. You can change things. You don't have to take the plunge from your existing company to a new company; you can decide now that you will stay put, but *create* a new kind of organization in-house. This is the essence of great leadership. It involves defining a new reality and then of making it happen. It can only happen if you have the courage, skills, and internal reputation to pull it off. Deciding when to stay and build versus moving on may be the most important career decision you make!

SUMMARY COMMENTS

In this chapter we have reviewed the challenges Japanese companies are facing as they move from an export-orientation to a more borderless global approach to business. We identified a number of steps that companies and decision makers can take to assist in the transition. We addressed the challenges and merits of overcoming cognitive biases, adding diversity, changing policies for promoting people to the top levels of companies, and of taking a more systematic approach to global leadership development. In addition, we reviewed the challenges and opportunities that individual Japanese managers are facing during this period of uncertainty. We highlighted the importance of taking charge of their own career and personal development and of deciding the degree to which they might be motivated to follow others or play a leadership role in determining the future.

In the next chapter, we turn the tables and discuss lessons and recommendations for the rest of us. Just as the challenges for Japanese mangers may at times seem overwhelming, the future for American and European MNCs is neither easy nor is the path clear.

11

A CAUTIONARY TALE

At this point, if your company headquarters is in Oslo, New York, Madrid, Jakarta, Paris, Houston, or almost anywhere but Japan, it might be easy to feel comfortable, even smug, because of the challenges Japanese MNCs seem to face. This may come from a belief that if someone else is down, you must be up. But, harboring this belief would be a grave mistake. Anyone who personally experienced the peak of the Japanese economy in the late 1980s and then its fall, or anyone who was comfortable in 2007 but experienced the pain of 2009 after the economic meltdown of 2008 has to realize that nothing is secure. Much can change, and often quicker than we think. To quote a Chinese proverb, "As you climb the ladder of success, check occasionally to make sure it is leaning against the right wall."

In our view one of the key lessons from the rise and subsequent struggles of Japanese MNCs is that getting into deep organizational and financial trouble is often more analogous to catching a virus than receiving a blow from a prizefighter. Consider a virus after it enters the body. It grows and begins to spread. And yet initially the patient feels perfectly well. There is no pain. There is no fever. All is well. Until a slight cough appears. Perhaps it is just the air conditioning? Perhaps it is nothing? And then things start to go downhill. The headache begins. The chills start. The fever finally hits. Suddenly, there is no denying that you are sick, perhaps gravely ill. The good news is that in many cases the human body is successful at repelling these viral attacks. But sometimes a new illness pops up, something with unique characteristics for which the body is not prepared. And when this happens the consequences can be devastating.

As it is with a virus, so it is with competition, particularly for borderless global companies. Everything can feel wonderful with profits soaring and morale high. And then before you know it you are under attack in a part of the world you have barely heard of by a strange competitor you have never seen before. The competitor brings something new, unique, and unheard of to the equation. And like the early stages of an illness, you may be prone to ignore the mounting signs that perhaps not all is well. But also like a virus left unchecked, the consequences can be devastating.

In this chapter we offer some advice to those aspiring to escape the false belief that winning a few international battles guarantees victory in the global war. We start by sharing some observations geared to a sub-set of competitors who have built their current successes largely on the basis of a "follow the Japanese" approach to strategy. The largest group of these competitors come from developing countries like Korea, Taiwan, and increasingly China. We then expand our discussion to include lessons that firms from developed countries such as the United States, Germany, France, and the United Kingdom might incorporate.

A FEW WORDS OF CAUTION FOR THE "FOLLOW JAPAN" CROWD

After watching the Japanese juggernaut gain speed in the 1960s, 70s, and 80s, it isn't surprising that a lot of companies took note, liked what they saw, and decided to play by a similar game. And some have done a pretty good job at it. For example, Korean, Taiwanese, and Chinese firms have all added firms to the *Fortune Global 500* list over the past 15 years. Many firms in these and other developing countries share some striking similarities with Japanese MNCs of the past:

- Support from powerful government bureaucracies,
- Important protection at home from foreign competitors because of unique domestic cultural, linguistic, and regulatory hurdles,
- The ability to import and leverage foreign technology,
- Low labor and other factor costs that facilitate manufacturing scale economies, and
- Open export markets and external demand for exported goods.

Companies such as Haier (Chinese manufacturer of white goods), HTC (Taiwan-based manufacturer of mobile phones), and Techtronic Industries (Hong Kong manufacturer of household appliances and power tools) have thus far prospered mightily using strategies that closely resemble those employed by some of the most successful Japanese companies.

The good news for many of these companies is that they started the process of globalizing later than the Japanese. This allowed them to learn from the Japanese, to copy what worked, and to introduce new practices that perhaps the Japanese overlooked. And we see some evidence that lessons are being learned. Korean companies including LG and Hyundai have had some of the most ambitious global leadership development budgets in the world. In 1995, for example, LG's chairman, Boon Moo Koo announced global expansion plans that required the addition of 1,400 new *global* leaders by 2005, half of whom would be non-Korean. In a move to broaden learning, and increase local responsiveness, Hyundai in 2004 announced plans to locate its Hyundai America Technical Center Headquarters in Michigan, employing 750 people,[1] one of many investments in the United States and Europen Union. In 2006, Techtronic purchased Hoover from Whirlpool in a move to strengthen its US-based floor care business and buttress its other brands including Ryobi, Homelite, and Dirt Devil. Chinese companies have likewise made progress at diversifying their geographic and cultural competencies, often through joint ventures. In 1997, Shanghai Automotive Industry Corporation in China signed two JVs with US-based General Motors. One JV focused on automobile production, the other—the Pan Asia Technical Automotive Center—focused on engineering and design. In 2006, Pan Asia received the go-ahead to design what would become known in the United States as the Buick LaCrosse, a sleek, highly acclaimed mid-size car introduced in 2009. The effort has become a case study in effective cross-cultural cooperation and learning.

Clearly, these and other case studies are impressive. Our question is, "Will these companies be the norm or the exception?" Will MNCs from these emerging markets proactively embrace the diversification of human capital needed to become global or will they let the success of exports led by more homogeneous leadership teams lull them into a false sense of security? Like Japanese MNCs, many of these firms are headquartered in countries that for historical, cultural, and linguistic reasons have low exposure to and interaction with foreigners. For example, in a 2008 survey, 42% of Korean respondents reported that they had *never* once spoken with a foreigner.[2] Outside the major cities, most Chinese may live their entire lives never having met a foreigner.

With few exceptions, companies throughout Asia and the developing world have just started to fight the "real" battles of globalization. We illustrate the complexity of the challenges they face with three somewhat disparate examples.

The first specific example is Samsung. Despite Samsung's impressive sales of electronics, including plasma TVs, in the United States its entire senior management team is Korean; and eight of their nine corporate board members are Koreans. If this lack of diversity continues, based on the Japanese experience, we would anticipate Samsung to experience significant globalization and growth challenges over the next 10–20 years.

The second general example comes from Taiwanese manufacturers. While manufacturers in Taiwan have become exceptional exporters, we see a lack of needed diversity in senior managers. For example, a 2007 study of 100 subsidiaries of Taiwanese multinationals found a sharp and dominant "home country" effect in terms of strategic decision making and many core human resource practices.[3] Were this to continue, we predict that Taiwanese firms, like the Japanese before them, will face serious long-term growth challenges, particularly if they want to shift away from commodity manufacturing.

Our final example comes to us from PR China. In 2005, the Chinese National Offshore Oil Company (CNOOC) attempted a hostile takeover of Unocal. It was a public relations disaster and ended in failure and loss of face for the company's executives. Pundits near and far panned CNOOC's executives—the pride of China—for their naivety and complete disconnection with US politics and public perceptions. Although they had deep pockets, years of China-centric thinking and a complete lack of senior management diversity doomed the takeover attempt before it even got off the ground. Had they succeeded in the takeover, we can't help but wonder if the acquisition would have followed the pattern of the Japanese purchase of Rockefeller Plaza in New York: Pay a giant price for prestige. Have few post-acquisition plans to leverage the purchase. Infuriate the public. Then, a few years later walk away looking awfully foolish, having destroyed shareholder value in the process.

Each of these examples illustrates the kinds of problems companies from developing countries face as they globalize. In our view, there are three fundamental lessons that MNCs in developing countries should take from the Japanese. First, by all means continue to grow and continue to push and leverage exports. However, remember that growth through exports will take you only so far. At some point, international operations will be required and that "what got you here won't get you there." As a consequence, rather than view profits generated through exports in isolation, view them as investment funding for future growth through international expansion. Second, in adding international operations, it is critical to get "home-country nationals" *out* (expatriation) but equally important to get foreign nationals *in* (inpatriation). Building up global leadership takes years and therefore the global leadership development process has to start long before global leaders are needed. Third, because truly global operations require truly global leaders, recognizing that diversity at the top of the organization is essential. Without it you cannot obtain the depth of insights and source of wisdom that will improve overall decision-making quality and lead to sustainable, prosperous, long-term global success. While simple in theory, this may be the most difficult of all recommendations for decision makers to embrace. Don't consider it giving up power, think of it as the price to pay for building a global organization. On this, we are reminded of what Winston Churchill once said, "a pessimist sees the difficulty in every opportunity; an optimist sees the opportunity in every difficulty."

LESSONS FOR EXPERIENCED MNCs

Many firms have been international for a long time—working in multiple foreign countries for decades. For executives in these firms, it may seem that there is little to learn from the experience of Japanese MNCs. We take a different perspective and believe there are at least three lessons to learn.

Building structural flexibility

One of the central challenges observed in many Japanese MNCs is that they are built up and oriented around a large, export structure. When it was time to move to a more international structure, many could simply not overcome 20–40 years of organizational inertia. We see the same phenomenon but at a different stage for many developed MNCs. Companies such as Exxon, BASF, P&G, Philips, Coca Cola, and Michelin have had operations in scores of countries for decades. They have built up large, international organizations. However, in many of these firms, the international operations are like planets spinning around the central sun, whether that sun is located in Irving, Ludwigshafen, Cincinnati, Amsterdam, Atlanta, or Paris. Transitioning from international to global operations requires a more distributed nerve network and a brain that doesn't reside strictly at the head-office.[4] While a "distributed nerve network" and a "nodal rather than central brain" structure sounds provocative, it is difficult to find working examples of this new business model. Which is why we think looking outside business to the military may offer some insights.

Lessons from the military

Conventional armies have long been organized around divisions, regiments, and squadrons. Controlling individuals within the organization requires a tight vertical chain of command. The US Army was built on a command and control structure that included no less than ten different ranks for commissioned officers—from second Lieutenant to General—and ten enlisted ranks—from Private to Sergeant Major. In total, twenty layers exist between top and bottom.

There is nothing like a shock to call into question past models and the need for new ones. For the US military, the terrorists attacks of 9/11 in 2001 did just that. In looking at the structure of networks such as al-Qaida, John Arzuilia, a professor at the Naval Postgraduate School in Monterey, California, described the need to shift the thinking from the "large and few" to the "small and the many." He and others argued for a new approach that would utilize units organized similar in many ways to terrorist cells and street gangs, but with the network ability to draw on the enormous resources of the global US military.

At the heart of the "small and the many" thinking is the US Special Forces. The basic operating unit in the Green Beret Special Forces is the Detachment-A or what has become known as A-Team. Each A-Team is composed of only 12 men. Six A-Team Detachments make up a Company.

Each A-Team operates as a self-contained unit under the direction of a captain. Second in command is a warrant officer followed by ten sergeant-level non-commissioned officers. Each member of the detachment has a functional responsibility that contributes to a breadth of skills critical to the team's independence: weapons, engineering and demolition, medicine, communications, and operations and intelligence. Furthermore, all team members are cross-trained to ensure redundancy in the case of an injury or where double-duty is required. Joining the Special Forces is no easy task. The rigor of the training means that less than 10% of soldiers who apply eventually make the cut; applicants are amongst the best qualified in the military. Those who do get in are not only physically fit but also emotionally strong. They are also older and better educated than most regular army soldiers.

In order to blend in and maximize intelligence gathering, A-Team soldiers operating in Afghanistan are encouraged to grow their hair and beards out. They live in unmarked compounds and have shunned heavy equipment that would slow them down and draw attention. They are trained in cross-cultural sensitivities, foreign language—usually Arabic—and the technologies of the battlefield. The more they look and think like locals the better.

Combined with this small and local capabilities are a global network of satellite communications, laser range finders, GPS targeting devices, and a global R&D and asset production capability (that is, planes, bombs, etc.) that allow A-Teams to feed planes or unmanned drones precise coordinates based on real-time intelligence. When it all works as planned, enemy forces don't stand a chance.

Other countries—Britain, Germany, France—have similar organizations. Whatever the nationality, Special Forces have adopted common approaches. They

- organize into small, cohesive units,
- staff units with people who have a wide range of skills—like a fast moving army in miniature,
- select only the most qualified recruits,
- work tirelessly at keeping skills sharp and focused,
- maximize the operating autonomy of the unit,
- employ world-class technology,
- blend in, learn the language and terrain, and get as close as possible to the local population,
- in times of need, call on the heavy resources of the army.

Lessons for business

Just as the military had to evolve its structure in order to deal with conventional battles and the new threat and structure of terrorist cells, global organizations need to manage the transition from international to global competition. Global competition is not about abandoning "conventional" tools such as mega factories, global distribution, and tight command and control systems, but it is rather about adding "Special Forces" capabilities.

In practice, this means creating and using teams of highly skilled leaders that can be installed in outlying markets. Like A-Teams, they will act with considerable autonomy in making local decisions that are networked into the global organization and objectives. For example, Coca-Cola leverages its "conventional army" of centrally controlled brand, logo, finance, and deep pocketed R&D but at the same time utilizes a more "special forces" approach to decisions including local bottling and distribution partners, container sizes, and product forms—dispensing machines versus cans versus bottles—sugar type and sweetness, level of carbonization, etc.[5]

Building diversity

Most Japanese firms have struggled with the addition of leader diversity and this has restricted their progression along the path to globalization. As we look at more developed MNCs, this risk and challenge do not seem to be fully recognized or met. While American, German, French, British, and other MNCs seem to be ahead of their Japanese counterparts in the diversity of leaders at the top of their organizations, "revenue diversity" (that is, the geographical origins of sales) is far ahead of leader diversity. Much more needs to be done on the diversity front.

In a global context, having a broad mix of people is critical because only through diversity can companies accomplish two primary tasks: (1) developing a deep understanding of local conditions, including customer needs, government policy, labor conditions, etc., and (2) establishing and maintaining meaningful, personal relationships with these constituents. Without these connections even the best products will quickly lose their appeal and efforts to truly globalize will falter.

Achieving leader diversity requires that companies follow a two-step approach. First, firms need to build bench-strength in overseas affiliates. This includes populating overseas affiliates with talented locals and culturally adaptable expatriates. Second, firms need to ensure that these folks are fully integrated with the top decision makers of the firm.

The implications of mixed diversity for management are quite profound. First, as companies become truly global in their approach to business, the composition of their management ranks should move *directionally* in favor of the demographic realities of their customer base. We are not suggesting that because 5% of your customers are French, you should have a quota that 5% of your managers also should be French. Nor are we suggesting your company walk away from its heritage or country of origin. But directionally, the number of "foreigners" in key leadership positions in the company will need to rise *a lot* in most companies. So too will the number of non-national CEOs and non-national board members. In our estimation, in the coming years companies will begin to experience significant negative consequences if the ranks of their home country national upper managers remain greater than twice the size of the home market relative to overall company sales.

However, simply adding nationalities to the leadership team is not sufficient. Current leaders must work to ensure that the future leaders are not just carbon copies of themselves with different passports. Diversity should extend to differences in educational backgrounds, gender, skills, personal values, etc.

As university professors, we often work with or around company recruiters who make their annual pilgrimage to the campus. Most come looking for a particular "type" of candidate. For some this means that they will only recruit the top students from the top business schools. For others, it means that they must have a certain "look" or philosophy about business. Because we often taught "core" courses in the MBA program, recruiters would sometimes approach us privately and ask us to help in profiling potential hires. One company—a leading high-technology company—specifically wanted the names of students in the second quartile of one of our classes. Why? They felt that top quartile students were more arrogant and less tractable than second quartile students. Whether true or not, they were looking for people to turn into clones of themselves. Needless to say, we declined the interviewer's request for the list.

Diversity must be built and *managed*. It won't just happen. And it isn't just a matter of casting a wider net when looking for recruits. It also takes systems to move people around. It takes systems to develop managers and give them the breadth of experiences that will encourage them to accept and appreciate diversity in *their* employees. Few employees are perfect; everyone needs improvements and development plays a central role in meeting the diversity challenge. On this dimension, development has less to do with organizing diversity training classes and much more to do with giving people the kind of cross-cultural experiences that will enable them to personally value diversity in their teams.

Investing in speedy transitions

If bringing in new and different people is critical, if giving existing leaders new and different experiences are essential to creating the needed diversity for global business, then managing these transitions effectively is also vital. We know from both experience and significant research that simply moving people from one country to another or simply throwing a bunch of people together from different nationalities does not automatically create functional diversity.[6]

What characterizes every transition is that once the transition has begun, there is a period when value is actually destroyed. An experienced manager in France simply has no idea how to lead people in China. Similarly, an experienced technical leader, simply has no idea how to manage a team composed of external relations, marketing, production, HR, and technical service folks. Because of the "newness" of the context, cross-cultural skills are weak. In one study of management transitions, it took new managers an average of just over six months before the amount of net new value they created exceeded the amount of value consumed during the early days of their appointments.[7] Transitioning entire organizations is bound to take much longer.

Clearly, some transitions are more difficult than others. For an American, moving to Canada will usually require less transitional adjustments than moving to Indonesia. Similarly, establishing a single function JV in one country will require far less adjustment time than setting up a global partnership involving five different functions. Irrespective of the challenges, managing transitions effectively means shrinking the time it takes to move from the negative part of the equation to the positive side.

Speeding the process

Our research and that of many others clearly demonstrate that all transitions involve ambiguity and that selecting people who have a high tolerance for ambiguity and who work to transcend seemingly opposing objectives is one of the smartest things organizations can do to speed up the transition process.[8]

Building skills in-house

Despite research that shows that an increasing number of companies are committed to globalizing their activities, relatively few do much to systematically develop their leaders.[9] Most approach global leadership development in an ad-hoc manner. Given what is at stake, we suggest this is a shortsighted, penny wise, pound foolish approach.

Effective global leadership development should include multiple components: work on cross-cultural teams, travel, international assignments, and formal executive training programs. Each plays an important but different role in developing the "whole" person. And each can play a different role at different stages in careers. Key to making this work is developing an architecture of global leadership development for the company as a whole, with separate development initiatives organized for different levels of managers in the organization. The goal should ultimately be the delivery of development activities just *before* they are needed—not three years later! As a result, development activities have to coincide closely with key transitions—organizationally or in the lives of individual managers.

FINAL COMMENTS

While the global sun may be setting on Japanese MNCs, no one is immune to the decline or to the globalization challenges that lie ahead. Borderless global business will require a very different kind of leadership; one that is "passport blind." By this we mean that current top executives must increasingly focus on the quality and capability of future leaders regardless of the country in which those future leaders were born or have citizenship.

For the foreseeable future, borderless global competition will mean both thinking and acting globally, while also thinking and acting locally. No nationality has cornered the market on this duality of global business. As a consequence, firms that want to transition from domestic, to export, to regional, and to global business must identify and develop the best talent wherever they can find it and expose that talent to the many peoples of the world and the complexities of global commerce.

In addition, top executives must look for the best talent wherever in the world they can find it and must find talent in all the various corners of the world because the world is not going to meld into a homogeneous global marketplace, devoid of significant differences by region, country, or even district within a country within our lifetime. We do not envision a day in the near future when Greeks will drop Greek as their national language or forget their specific culture and history and adopt some new Euro-lingua and Euro-identity; nor do we anticipate the French, German, Italians, or Spaniards doing so. We see no compelling evidence that Indonesians will soon give up their traditional songs in favor of ones from China or that Vietnamese will wholesale substitute their long-lived culinary tastes for those of India.

As a consequence of these facts, no global company can afford to have all senior executives primarily from that company's home country.

Additionally, no global company or one with global aspirations can afford to have a leadership pipeline that doesn't draw talent in and develop it from all corners of the world. Failure on both of these fronts will result in a senior leadership team that simply does not have the diversity of experience, networks, perspective, attitude, education, emotions, etc. to match the diversity of our global marketplace. Fundamentally, it is this lack of diversity at the top of Japanese firms and the lack of diversity in their leadership pipelines that have stymied their progression into the borderless global stage of development and has caused them in relative terms to fall on all the major global rankings.

Japanese firms may yet have brighter days ahead, but it is our prediction that these days will not come without major changes in the people who are targeted for development as leaders as well as changes in how these future global leaders are developed. Many non-Japanese MNCs from developing or developed economies may have an easier time transitioning from early stages to the borderless global stage of business, but we predict it will not be without becoming passport blind relative to who they identify and develop as global leaders.

NOTES

CHAPTER 2 – FOLLOW THE YELLOW BRICK ROAD, PART 1

1 Dunning, J., "Globalization and the theory of MNE activity," in N. Hood and S. Young (eds.), *The Globalization of Multinational Enterprise.* London: Macmillan, 1999. See also, Toyne, B. and Nigh, D. *International Business: An Emerging View.* Columbia, SC: University of South Carolina Press, 1997.

2 Morrison, A. J. and Roth, K., "The regional solution: An alternative to globalization." *Transnational Corporations,* 1 (2), 1992, pp. 37–55.

3 Ghemawat, P., "Regional strategies for global leadership." *Harvard Business Review,* December 2005, pp. 98–108.

4 Ghemawat, P., "Regional strategies for global leadership." *Harvard Business Review,* December 2005, pp. 98–108.

5 Hunt, L., Martin, T., Rosenwein, B., Hsia, R. et al., *The Making of the West, Peoples and Cultures.* Vol. C. 3rd ed. Boston: Bedford/ St. Martin's, 2009, Pp. 712–713.

6 Beasley, William G., *The Meiji Restoration.* California: Stanford University Press, 1972; Wolf Mendl, *Japan and South East Asia: From the Meiji Restoration to 1945.* London: Taylor & Francis, 2001.

7 Johnson, Chalmers A., *Miti and the Japanese Miracle: The Growth of Industrial Policy, 1925–1975.* California: Stanford University Press, 1982; Howe, Christopher, *The Origins of Japanese Trade Supremacy: Development and Technology in Asia from 1540 to the Pacific War.* Illinois: University of Chicago Press, 1999.

8 http://www.uaw.org/about/uawmembership.html Accessed September 20, 2009.

9 Japan Bureau of Statistics, Actual Conditions of Foreign Affiliates 1976–2002.

10 Syndaram, Anant K. and Black, J. Stewart, "The Honda-Yamaha War," *The International Business Environment.* New Jersey: Prentice-Hall, 1995, pp. 306–311.

11 Hofstede, Geert, *Cultures and Organizations.* New York: McGraw-Hill, 1991.

12 Miyashita, Kenichi and Russell, David, *Keiretsu: Inside the Hidden Japanese Conglomerates.* New York: McGaw-Hill, 1994.

13 Holstein, W., Treece, J., Crock, S., and Armstrong, L., "Mighty Mitsubishi is on the Move," *Business Week,* September 24, 1990, pp. 98–107. See also, "The main movers in Japan's biggest business groups," *Fortune,* July 15, 1991, p. 81.

14 Pascale, R. and Athos, A., *The Art of Japanese Management.* New York: Warner Books, 1981, pp. 190–191.

15 Miyashita, Kenichi and Russell, David W., *Keiretsu: Inside the Hidden Japanese Conglomerates.* New York: McGraw-Hill, 1994.

16 For more on the role of MITI in Japanese economic development, see Vestal, J. *Planning for Change: Industrial Policy and Japanese Economic Development, 1945–1990.* Oxford: Clarendon Press, 1993; Johnson, Chalmers A., *Miti and the Japanese Miracle: The Growth of Industrial Policy, 1925–1975.* California: Stanford University Press, 1982.

17 Yoshimura, Noboru and Anderson, Philip, *Inside the Kaisha.* Massachusetts: Harvard Business School Press, 1997; Miyashita, Kenichi and Russell, David W., *Keiretsu: Inside the Hidden Japanese Conglomerates.* New York: McGraw-Hill, 1994.

18 Yoshimura, Noboru and Anderson, Philip, *Inside the Kaisha.* Massachusetts: Harvard Business School Press, 1997.

CHAPTER 3 – FOLLOW THE YELLOW BRICK ROAD, PART 2

1 Stueck, William (ed.), *The Korean War in World History.* Kentucky: The University Press of Kentucky, 2004.

2 Ralston, D., Gustafson, D., Cheung, F., and Terpstra, R., "Eastern values: A comparison of US, Hong Kong and PRC managers." *Journal of Applied Psychology,* 77, 1992, pp. 664–671.

3 For additional reading on the development of culture, see Hofstede, G., *Cuture's Consequences: International Differences in Work-Related Values.* Newburry Park, CA: Sage, p. 1080. Also see, Ronen, S. and Shenkar, O., "Clustering Countries on attitudinal dimensions: A review and synthesis." *Academy of Management Review,* 10 (3), 1985, pp. 435–454.

4 For more on the challenges of integrating globally diverse cultures, see Yip, G. *Total Global Strategy: Managing for Worldwide Competitive Advantage.* New Jersey: Prentice-Hall, 1992.

5 Taylor, J., *Shadows of the Rising Sun: A Critical View of the "Japanese Miracle."* 1983. New York: WilliamMarrow & Co.

6 Drucker, P. "Japan's choice." *Foreign Affairs,* 65 (5), 1987, pp. 923–941.

7 Rowley, Ian, "A tough ride for Japan's carmakers," *BusinessWeek,* August 31, 2006 http://www.businessweek.com/globalbiz/content/aug2006.

8   Genzberger, Christine, *Japan Business: The Portable Encyclopedia for Doing Business with Japan.* Washington D.C.: World Trade Press, 1994.

9   Zeiler, Thomas W., *Free Trade, Free World: The Advent of GATT.* North Carolina: UNC Press, 1999.

10 Ibid.

11 Morrison, A. J., "Globalization and the Strategies of Transnational Corporations." Presentation at the High Level Symposium on the Contribution of TNCs to Growth and Development in Latin American and the Caribbean, United Nations Conference on Trade and Development, Santiago, Chile, 1992.

12 Knight, G., "International marketing blunders by American firms in Japan: Some lessons for management." *Journal of International Marketing,* 3 (4), 1995, pp. 107–129.

13 As cited by Boone, D., "Analytical review: The big three: Masters of their own fate in Japan?" *JAMA Forum: Journal of the Japan Automobile Manufacturer's Association,* August 1994, pp. 7–11.

14 For more on the Betty Crocker story, see Fields, G., *From Bonzai to Levis.* New York: Macmillan, 1983. Also, see "Learning how to please the baffling Japanese." *Fortune,* October 5, 1981, pp. 122–126.

15 Yang, C., "Demystifying Japanese management practices." *Harvard Business Review,* November–December 1984, 62, pp. 172–182.

16 Murphy, R. T., "Power without purpose: The crisis of Japanese global financial dominance." *Harvard Business Review,* March–April, 1989, 67, pp. 71–83.

17 Wood, C., *The Bubble Economy: Japan's Extraordinary Speculative Boom of the "80's and the Dramatic Bust of the '90."* New York: The Atlantic Monthly Press, 1992.

18 Murphy, T., "Power without purpose: The crisis of Japan's global financial dominance." *Harvard Business Review,* March–April, 1989, pp. 71–83.

19 Ibid., p. 72.

CHAPTER 4 – A BRAVE NEW WORLD

1   Honda Annual Report 2008.

2   Toyota Annual Report 2008.

3   "Toyota falters in booming China." *Wall Street Journal,* May 8, 2009.

4   Hamel, Gary and Prahalad, C. K., *Competing for the Future.* Massachusetts: Harvard Business School Press, 1994.

5   Kim, W. Chan and Mauborgne, Renée, *Blue Ocean Strategy.* Massachusetts: Harvard Business School Press, 2005.

6   Kelley, Tom and Littman, Jonathan, *The Ten Faces of Innovation: IDEO's Strategies for Beating the Devil's Advocate & Driving Creativity Throughout Your Organization.* New York: Currency/Doubleday, 2005.

7   Govindarajan, Vijay and Trimble, Chris, *Ten Rules for Strategic Innovators.* Massachusetts: Harvard Business Press, 2005.

8   Fleming, Lee, "Breakthroughs and the 'long tail' of innovation." *Sloan Management Review,* Fall 2007, pp 69–74.

9   Cohn, Jeffrey, Katzenbach, Jon and Vlak, Gus, "Finding and grooming breakthrough innovators." *Harvard Business Review,* Dec. 1, 2008; Hargadon, Andrew and Sutton, Robert , "Building a innovation factory." *Harvard Business Review,* May 1, 2000.

10 Black, J. Stewart, Morrison, Allen J., and Gregersen, Hal B., *Global Explorers: The Next Generation of Leaders.* New York: Routledge, 1999.

CHAPTER 5 – CURVE BALL

1   Simon, Herbert Alexander, *Administrative Behavior: A Study of Decision-making Processes in Administrative Organizations.* New York: Free Press, 1997.

2   Hofstede, Geert, *Cultures and Organizations.* New York: McGraw-Hill, 1991.

3   www.isuzu.co.jp/world/investor/fact/history.html Accessed October 31, 2009.

4   For more on the history of Isuzu, see "Isuzu History," http://www.edmunds. com/isuzu/history.html Accessed October 31, 2009.

5   "Isuzu quitting U.S. car market," *Los Angeles Times.* Retrieved on January 1, 2008.

CHAPTER 6 – BARBARIANS AT THE GATE

1   Black, J. Stewart, Gregersen, Hal B., Mendenhall, Mark E., and Stroh, Linda K., *Globalizing People through International Assignments.* Massachusetts: Addison-Wesley, 1999.

2   Kawakami, K., "The typical Japanese factory," in T. Abo (ed.), *Hybrid Factory: The Japanese Production System in the United States.* England: Oxford University Press, 1994, pp. 58–81; Kopp, R., *The Rice-Paper Ceiling.* California: Stone Bridge Press, 1994; Peterson, R. B., Sargent,J., Napier, N., and Shim, W. S., "Corporate expatriate HRM policies, internationalization, and performance of the world's largest MNCs." *Management International Review,* 36, pp. 215–230, 1996.

3   Kopp, R., *The Rice-Paper Ceiling.* California: Stone Bridge Press, 1994; Peterson, R. B., Sargent, J., Napier, N., and Shim, W. S., "Corporate expatriate HRM

policies, internationalization, and performance of the world's largest MNCs." *Management International Review*, 36, pp. 215–230, 1996.

4   Pucik, V., "The challenges of globalization: The strategic role of local managers in Japanese-owned US subsidiaries," in N. Campbell and F. Burton (eds.), *Japanese Multinationals: Strategies and Management in the Global Kaisha*. New York: Routledge, 1999, pp. 218–239 .

5   Nielsen, Sabina and Nielsen, Bo Bernhard, "The effects Of top management team and board nationality diversity and compensation systems on firm performance." *Academy of Management Proceedings*, 2006; Carpenter, Mason and Fredrickson, James, "Top management teams, global strategic posture, and the moderating role of uncertainty." *Academy of Management Journal*, 44 (3), 2001, pp. 533–545; Carpenter, Mason A., Sanders, Wm. Gerard, and Gregersen, Hal B., "Internationalization and firm governance." *Academy of Management Journal*, 44 (3), 2001, pp. 493–511.

6   Ruigrok, Winfried and Greve, Peder, "The Rise of the International Market for Executive Labor," SCALA Discussion Paper 7, 2007.

CHAPTER 7 – WATER, WATER EVERYWHERE, BUT NOT A DROP TO DRINK

1   Pollock, David C., and Reken, Ruth E. Van, *Third Culture Kids: The Experience of Growing Up Among Worlds*. London: Nicholas Brealey Publishing, 2001; Trawick-Smith, Jeffrey W., *Early Childhood Development: A Multicultural Perspective*. Ohio: Merrill, 1999; Brooks-Gunn, Jeanne, Fuligni, Allison Sidle, and Berlin, Lisa, *Early Child Development in the 21st Century: Profiles of Current Research Initiatives*. New York: Teachers College Press, 2003.

2   Black, J. Stewart, "O Kaerinasai: Factors related to Japanese repatriation adjustment." *Human Relations*, 47, 1994, 1489–1508; Black, J. Stewart, "Factors related to the adjustment of Japanese expatriate managers in America." *Research in Personnel and Human Resources Management* (Supplement V.2, *International Human Resource Management*), Greenwich, CT: JAI Press, 1990, pp. 109–125.

CHAPTER 8 – A TALE OF TWO CITIES

1   http://www.answers.com/topic/the-daiei-inc Accessed October 3, 2009; Butterfield, Fox, "Japan's retailing colossus," *New York Times*, November 3, 1974; "Daiei's discount empire prospers," *World Business Weekly*, January 12, 1981; Holden, Ted, "A retail rebel has the establishment quaking," *Business Week*, April 1, 1991, pp. 39–40.

2   *Fortune Global 500* list 1995.

3   "Seven-eleven Japan to overtake Daiei as top retailer," *AsiaPulse News*, April 24, 2000.

4   "Daiei president denies insider trading," *Daily Yomiuri,* October 4, 2000; "Daiei founder steps down as chairman," *AsiaPulse News,* October 11, 2000.

5   "Japan's Daiei Group to sell Lawson shares to Mitsubishi Group," *AsiaPulse News,* February 22, 2001.

6   "Hewlett-Packard president may take ailing Daiei's helm," *Japan Times,* Friday, April 15, 2005.

7   "Marubeni names exec to head Daiei," *Japan Times,* Thursday, Aug. 24, 2006.

8   "Aeon executive takes Daiei helm," *Japan Times,* Friday, May 25, 2007.

9   "Pro clubs back Daiei Hawks sale to Softbank," *Japan Times,* Tuesday, Nov. 16, 2004.

10   http://www.carrefour.com/cdc/group/history/ Accessed April 7, 2009.

11   Nakamura, Akemi, "Retail chains under siege; Foreign giants enter sans cumbersome middlemen," *Japan Times,* Thursday, Dec. 7, 2000.

12   "Carrefour chief takes aim at Japanese market," *Japan Times,* Friday, Dec. 8, 2000; "Thousands rush doors as Carrefour hits Japan," *Japan Times,* Saturday, Dec. 9, 2000.

13   Goda, Eiryo, "Can Carrefour succeed in Japan?" http://www.jmrlsi.co.jp/english/case/jmarket/2001/02_carrefour.html Accessed October 31, 2009.

14   http://www.carrefour.com/docroot/groupe/C4com/Pièces%20jointes/ Communiqués %20financiers/japon100305en.pdf Accessed October 31, 2009.

15   Carrefour Annual Report 2005.

16   Carrefour Annual Report 2007.

17   Carrefour Press Release November 18th, 2008.

18   Carrefour Press Release November 18th, 2008.

CHAPTER 9 – THE INCREDIBLE SHRINKING JAPAN

1   Japan Bureau of Statistics, 2008; Ishikawa, Tatsuya, *Population Decrease, Aging, and Japan's Long-Term Economic Outlook to 2050.* Economic Research Group, 2002; *Demographic Change and the Asian Economy,* Japan Center for Economic Research, 2002.

2   National Institute of Population and Social Security Research, http://www.ipss.go.jp/index-e.html Accessed April 15, 2009.

3   Japan Bureau of Statistics, 2008; Ishikawa, Tatsuya, *Population Decrease, Aging, and Japan's Long-Term Economic Outlook to 2050.* Economic Research Group, 2002.

4 Jorgenson, Dale and Nomura, Koji, "The industry origins of the US–Japan productivity gap," Japan Project Meeting, June 26–27, Tokyo, Japan, 2007.

CHAPTER 10 – SO WHAT ARE THE JAPANESE TO DO?

1 For more on the risks of promoting unrealistic recommendations, see Courtney, H. *20/20 Foresight: Crafting Strategy in an Uncertain World.* Massachusetts: Harvard Business School Press, 2001.

2 Barker, J., *Paradigms: The Business of Discovering the Future.* New York: HarperCollins, 1992.

3 As quoted in Harding, R., "Japan's export status hit by Sharp," *Financial Times* (Asia), April 9, 2009, p. 1.

4 Marks, M. and Mirvis, P., "Making mergers and acquisitions work: Strategic and psychological preparation." *Academy of Management Executive,* May, 15 (2), 2001, pp. 80–92.

5 See Tudor, A., "The international investor: Japan's unlikely shareholder advocate," *Wall Street Journal* (Europe), April 9, 2009.

6 Doz, Y. and Prahalad, C. K., "Quality of management: An emerging source of global competitive advantage," in N. Hood and J. Vahlne, *Strategies in Global Competition.* New York: Croom Helm, 1988.

7 Black, S., Morrison, A., and Gregersen, H., *Global Explorers: The Next Generation of Leaders.* New York: Routledge, 1999.

CHAPTER 11 – A CAUTIONARY TALE

1 "New Hyundai R & D Facility to Create 751 High Tech Jobs." Press release, Office of the Governor (Michigan), April 16, 2004.

2 Sang-Hun, Choe, "South Korea struggles with Race," *New York Times,* November 1, 2009, http://www.nytimes.com/2009/11/02/world/asia/02race Accessed November 2, 2009.

3 Chang, Y., Wilkinson, A., and Mellahi, K., "HRM strategies and MNCs from emerging economies in the UK." *European Business Review,* 19 (5), 2007, pp. 404–419.

4 Hedlund, G., "The hypermodern MNC—A heterarchy." *Human Resource Management*, Spring, 1986, pp. 9–35.

5 For more on Coca-Cola's approach to globalization, see Kanter, R. M. and Dretler, T., "Global strategy and its impact on local operations." *Academy of Management Executive,* November 1998, pp. 60–68.

6   Black, S., Morrison, A., and Gregersen, H., *Global Explorers: The Next Generation of Leaders*. New York: Routledge, 1999.

7   For more on value destruction during the early stages of transition, see Watkins, M., *The First 90 Days*. Massachusetts: Harvard Business School Press, 2003.

8   Black, S., Morrison, A., and Gregersen, H., *Global Explorers: The Next Generation of Leaders*. New York: Routledge, 1999.

9   Black, S., Morrison, A., and Gregersen, H., *Global Explorers: The Next Generation of Leaders*. New York: Routledge, 1999.

INDEX